CONFRONTING GLOBAL WARMING

The Role of
the Government

CONFRONTING GLOBAL WARMING

The Role of the Government

Jacqueline Langwith

Michael E. Mann
Consulting Editor

WILLOW INTERNATIONAL LIBRARY

GREENHAVEN PRESS
A part of Gale, Cengage Learning

GALE
CENGAGE Learning

Detroit • New York • San Francisco • New Haven, Conn • Waterville, Maine • London

Christine Nasso, *Publisher*
Elizabeth Des Chenes, *Managing Editor*

© 2011 Greenhaven Press, a part of Gale, Cengage Learning

For more information, contact:

Greenhaven Press
27500 Drake Rd.
Farmington Hills, MI 48331-3535
Or you can visit our Internet site at
gale.cengage.com.

For product information and technology assistance, contact us at
Gale Customer Support, 1-800-877-4253.

For permission to use material from this text or product, submit all requests online at
www.cengage.com/permissions.

Further permissions questions can be e-mailed to permissionrequest@cengage.com

Every effort is made to ensure that Greenhaven Press accurately reflects the original intent of the authors. Every effort has been made to trace the owners of copyrighted material.

Cover Image © Alan Schein/Corbis and image copyright © JinYoung Lee, 2010, used under license from Shutterstock.com; leaf icon © iStockPhoto.com/domin_domin.

LIBRARY OF CONGRESS
CATALOGING-IN-PUBLICATION DATA

Langwith, Jacqueline.
  The role of the government / Jacqueline Langwith.
    p. cm. -- (Confronting global warming)
  Includes bibliographical references and index.
  ISBN 978-0-7377-4860-4 (hardcover)
  1. Environmental policy--United States. 2. Climatic changes--Government policy--United States. 3. Global warming--Government policy--United States. I. Title.
  GE180.R65 2010
  363.738'740561--dc2
                                          2010024975

Printed in the United States of America
1 2 3 4 5 6 7 14 13 12 11 10

Contents

Preface

> *"The warnings about global warming
> have been extremely clear for a long
> time. We are facing a global climate
> crisis. It is deepening. We are entering
> a period of consequences."*
> *Al Gore*

Still hotly debated by some, human-induced global warming is now accepted in the scientific community. Earth's average yearly temperature is getting steadily warmer; sea levels are rising due to melting ice caps; and the resulting impact on ocean life, wildlife, and human life is already evident. The human-induced buildup of greenhouse gases in the atmosphere poses serious and diverse threats to life on earth. As scientists work to develop accurate models to predict the future impact of global warming, researchers, policy makers, and industry leaders are coming to terms with what can be done today to halt and reverse the human contributions to global climate change.

Each volume in the Confronting Global Warming series examines the current and impending challenges the planet faces because of global warming. Several titles focus on a particular aspect of life—such as weather, farming, health, or nature and wildlife—that has been altered by climate change. Consulting the works of leading experts in the field, Confronting Global Warming authors present the current status of those aspects as they have been affected by global warming, highlight key future challenges, examine potential solutions for dealing with the results of climate change, and address the pros and cons of imminent changes and challenges. Other volumes in the series—such as those dedicated to the role of government, the role of industry, and the role of the individual—address the impact various facets of society can have on climate change. The result is a series that provides students and general-interest readers with a solid understanding of the worldwide ramifications of climate change and what can be done to help humanity adapt to changing conditions and mitigate damage.

Each volume includes:

- A descriptive **table of contents** listing subtopics, charts, graphs, maps, and sidebars included in each chapter
- Full-color **charts, graphs, and maps** to illustrate key points, concepts, and theories
- Full-color **photos** that enhance textual material
- **Sidebars** that provide explanations of technical concepts or statistical information, present case studies to illustrate the international impact of global warming, or offer excerpts from primary and secondary documents
- **Pulled quotes** containing key points and statistical figures
- A **glossary** providing users with definitions of important terms
- An annotated **bibliography** of additional books, periodicals, and Web sites for further research
- A detailed **subject index** to allow users to quickly find the information they need

The Confronting Global Warming series provides students and general-interest readers with the information they need to understand the complex issue of climate change. Titles in the series offer users a well-rounded view of global warming, presented in an engaging format. Confronting Global Warming not only provides context for how society has dealt with climate change thus far but also encapsulates debates about how it will confront issues related to climate in the future.

Foreword

Earth's climate is a complex system of interacting natural components. These components include the atmosphere, the ocean, and the continental ice sheets. Living things on earth—or, the biosphere—also constitute an important component of the climate system.

Natural Factors Cause Some of Earth's Warming and Cooling

Numerous factors influence Earth's climate system, some of them natural. For example, the slow drift of continents that takes place over millions of years, a process known as plate tectonics, influences the composition of the atmosphere through its impact on volcanic activity and surface erosion. Another significant factor involves naturally occurring gases in the atmosphere, known as greenhouse gases, which have a warming influence on Earth's surface. Scientists have known about this warming effect for nearly two centuries: These gases absorb outgoing heat energy and direct it back toward the surface. In the absence of this natural greenhouse effect, Earth would be a frozen, and most likely lifeless, planet.

Another natural factor affecting Earth's climate—this one measured on timescales of several millennia—involves cyclical variations in the geometry of Earth's orbit around the sun. These variations alter the distribution of solar radiation over the surface of Earth and are responsible for the coming and going of the ice ages every one hundred thousand years or so. In addition, small variations in the brightness of the sun drive minor changes in Earth's surface temperature over decades and centuries. Explosive volcanic activity, such as the Mount Pinatubo eruption in the Philippines in 1991, also affects Earth's climate. These eruptions inject highly reflective particles called aerosol into the upper part of the atmosphere, known as the stratosphere, where they can reside for a year or longer. These particles reflect some of the incoming sunlight back into space and cool Earth's surface for years at a time.

Human Progress Puts Pressure on Natural Climate Patterns

Since the dawn of the industrial revolution some two centuries ago, however, humans have become the principal drivers of climate change. The burning of fossil fuels—such as oil, coal, and natural gas—has led to an increase in atmospheric levels of carbon dioxide, a powerful greenhouse gas. And farming practices have led to increased atmospheric levels of methane, another potent greenhouse gas. If humanity continues such activities at the current rate through the end of this century, the concentrations of greenhouse gases in the atmosphere will be higher than they have been for tens of millions of years. It is the unprecedented rate at which we are amplifying the greenhouse effect, warming Earth's surface, and modifying our climate that causes scientists so much concern.

The Role of Scientists in Climate Observation and Projection

Scientists study Earth's climate not just from observation but also from a theoretical perspective. Modern-day climate models successfully reproduce the key features of Earth's climate, including the variations in wind patterns around the globe, the major ocean current systems such as the Gulf Stream, and the seasonal changes in temperature and rainfall associated with Earth's annual revolution around the sun. The models also reproduce some of the more complex natural oscillations of the climate system. Just as the atmosphere displays random day-to-day variability that we term "weather," the climate system produces its own random variations, on timescales of years. One important example is the phenomenon called El Niño, a periodic warming of the eastern tropical Pacific Ocean surface that influences seasonal patterns of temperature and rainfall around the globe. The ability to use models to reproduce the climate's complicated natural oscillatory behavior gives scientists increased confidence that these models are up to the task of mimicking the climate system's response to human impacts.

To that end, scientists have subjected climate models to a number of rigorous tests of their reliability. James Hansen of the NASA Goddard Institute for Space Studies performed a famous experiment back in 1988, when he subjected a climate model (one relatively primitive by modern standards) to possible future fossil fuel emissions scenarios. For the scenario that most closely matches actual emissions since then, the model's predicted course of global temperature increase shows an uncanny correspondence to the actual increase in temperature over the intervening two decades. When Mount Pinatubo erupted in the Philippines in 1991, Hansen performed another famous experiment. Before the volcanic aerosol had an opportunity to influence the climate (it takes several months to spread globally throughout the atmosphere), he took the same climate model and subjected it to the estimated atmospheric aerosol distribution. Over the next two years, actual global average surface temperatures proceeded to cool a little less than 1°C (1.8°F), just as Hansen's model predicted they would.

Given that there is good reason to trust the models, scientists can use them to answer important questions about climate change. One such question weighs the human factors against the natural factors to determine responsibility for the dramatic changes currently taking place in our climate. When driven by natural factors alone, climate models do not reproduce the observed warming of the past century. Only when these models are also driven by human factors—primarily, the increase in greenhouse gas concentrations—do they reproduce the observed warming. Of course, the models are not used just to look at the past. To make projections of future climate change, climate scientists consider various possible scenarios or pathways of future human activity.

The earth has warmed roughly 1°C since preindustrial times. In the "business as usual" scenario, where we continue the current course of burning fossil fuel through the twenty-first century, models predict an additional warming anywhere from roughly 2°C to 5°C (3.6°F to 9°F). The models also show that even if we were to stop fossil fuel burning today, we are probably committed to as much as 0.6°C additional warming because of the inertia of the climate system. This inertia ensures warming for a century to come, simply due to our greenhouse gas emissions thus far. This committed warming introduces a profound procrastination penalty for not taking immediate action. If we are to avert an additional warming of 1°C, which would bring the net warming to 2°C—often considered an appropriate threshold for defining dangerous human impact on our climate—we have to act almost immediately.

Long-Term Warming May Bring About Extreme Changes Worldwide

In the "business as usual" emissions scenario, climate change will have an array of substantial impacts on our society and the environment by the end of this century. Patterns of rainfall and drought are projected to shift in such a way that some regions currently stressed for water resources, such as the desert southwest of the United States and the Middle East, are likely to become drier. More intense rainfall events in other regions, such as Europe and the midwestern United States, could lead to increased flooding. Heat waves like the one in Europe in summer 2003, which killed more than thirty thousand people, are projected to become far more common. Atlantic hurricanes are likely to reach greater intensities, potentially doing far more damage to coastal infrastructure.

Furthermore, regions such as the Arctic are expected to warm faster than the rest of the globe. Disappearing Arctic sea ice already threatens wildlife, including polar bears and walruses. Given another 2°C warming (3.6°F), a substantial portion of the

Greenland ice sheet is likely to melt. This event, combined with other factors, could lead to more than 1 meter (about 3 feet) of sea-level rise by the end of the century. Such a rise in sea level would threaten many American East Coast and Gulf Coast cities, as well as low-lying coastal regions and islands around the world. Food production in tropical regions, already insufficient to meet the needs of some populations, will probably decrease with future warming. The incidence of infectious disease is expected to increase in higher elevations and in latitudes with warming temperatures. In short, the impacts of future climate change are likely to have a devastating impact on society and our environment in the absence of intervention.

Strategies for Confronting Climate Change

Options for dealing with the threats of climate change include both adaptation to inevitable changes and mitigation, or lessening, of those changes that we can still affect. One possible adaptation would be to adjust our agricultural practices to the changing regional patterns of temperature and rainfall. Another would be to build coastal defenses against the inundation from sea-level rise. Only mitigation, however, can prevent the most threatening changes. One means of mitigation that has been given much recent attention is geoengineering. This method involves perturbing the climate system in such a way as to partly or fully offset the warming impact of rising greenhouse gas concentrations. One geoengineering approach involves periodically shooting aerosol particles, similar to ones produced by volcanic eruptions, into the stratosphere—essentially emulating the cooling impact of a major volcanic eruption on an ongoing basis. As with nearly all geoengineering proposals, there are potential perils with this scheme, including an increased tendency for continental drought and the acceleration of stratospheric ozone depletion.

The only foolproof strategy for climate change mitigation is the decrease of greenhouse gas emissions. If we are to avert a dangerous 2°C increase relative to preindustrial times, we will probably need to bring greenhouse gas emissions to a peak within the coming years and reduce them well below current levels within the coming decades. Any strategy for such a reduction of emissions must be international and multipronged, involving greater conservation of energy resources; a shift toward alternative, carbon-free sources of energy; and a coordinated set of governmental policies that encourage responsible corporate and individual practices. Some contrarian voices argue that we cannot afford to take such steps. Actually, given the procrastination penalty of not acting on the climate change problem, what we truly cannot afford is to delay action.

Evidently, the problem of climate change crosses multiple disciplinary boundaries and involves the physical, biological, and social sciences. As an issue facing all of civilization, climate change demands political, economic, and ethical considerations. With the Confronting Global Warming series, Greenhaven Press addresses all of these considerations in an accessible format. In ten thorough volumes, the series covers the full range of climate change impacts (water and ice; extreme weather; population, resources, and conflict; nature and wildlife; farming and food supply; health and disease) and the various essential components of any solution to the climate change problem (energy production and alternative energy; the role of government; the role of industry; and the role of the individual). It is my hope and expectation that this series will become a useful resource for anyone who is curious about not only the nature of the problem but also about what we can do to solve it.

Michael E. Mann

Michael E. Mann is a professor in the Department of Meteorology at Penn State University and director of the Penn State Earth

System Science Center. In 2002 he was selected as one of the fifty leading visionaries in science and technology by Scientific American. *He was a lead author for the "Observed Climate Variability and Change" chapter of the Intergovernmental Panel on Climate Change (IPCC) Third Scientific Assessment Report, and in 2007 he shared the Nobel Peace Prize with other IPCC authors. He is the author of more than 120 peer-reviewed publications, and he recently coauthored the book* Dire Predictions: Understanding Global Warming *with colleague Lee Kump. Mann is also a co-founder and avid contributor to the award-winning science Web site RealClimate.org.*

CHAPTER 1

The Government and the Environment: Setting the Precedent

The climate is the ultimate public good. One of the basic concepts presented in introductory economic textbooks is that of the public good. In *Essentials of Economics*, Paul Krugman, Robin Wells, and Martha Olney describe a public good as "a good that is *nonexcludable* and *nonrival in consumption*."[1] A good is nonexcludable if the supplier cannot prevent consumption of the good by people who do not pay for it. For instance, if the United States, Britain, and a majority of countries reduce their greenhouse gas emissions and incur costs in so doing, and if their actions mitigate global warming, all countries benefit, even ones that did not reduce their emissions or incur any costs. The climate is nonrival in consumption because it can be enjoyed by people all over the planet at the same time and one person's enjoyment of it does not decrease the amount that can be enjoyed by others. The climate is a concern for governments because one of the roles of government is to provide for the public good. Past international treaties and U.S. environmental laws designed to deal with air pollution have helped shape the government's role in ensuring that the climate remains a public good for all to enjoy.

The Air Knows No Boundaries

Some of the first international environmental treaties involved issues of air pollution. One of the first international air pollution treaties was the Geneva Convention on Long-Range Transboundary Air Pollution, which was signed in Geneva, Switzerland, on November 13, 1979, by twenty-nine European countries, the United States, Canada, and the European Community. The treaty was based on the recognition that air pollution originating in one country was causing damage in another country. This concept was first recognized by Swedish chemist Svante Oden. In the 1960s, he began noticing that the pH of many Scandinavian lakes was dropping—the lakes were becoming acidic. Fish, underwater plants, and most aquatic animals cannot survive in acidic conditions. So, although the lakes looked beautiful and crystal clear, there was no life in them. Oden wondered how the lakes could become acidic. He hypothesized that acid rain was lowering the pH of the lakes, and the acidifying agent in the rain was coming from the far-off factories of other continental European countries and Britain. He called acid rain "an insidious chemical war."[2] Oden's hypothesis, although first disputed, came to be scientifically proven. In the 1970s, several studies confirmed that air pollutants could travel several thousands of miles in the air before falling back to the earth in precipitation. As a result of Oden's research, it was realized that sulfur dioxide (SO_2), and other acidic gases produced when fossil fuels are burned in power plants and factories, was being transported to Sweden, Denmark, and Norway from countries south of them, and then falling as rain, snow, or sleet. Soon it was discovered that acid rain was causing widespread environmental damage to forests and lakes and ruining buildings and stone monuments.

In their quest to reduce the impacts of acid rain, the Scandinavian countries began negotiating with Britain and other European countries under the auspices of the United Nations Economic Commission for Europe. The Geneva Convention on Long-Range Transboundary Air Pollution was born as a result of these negotiations. Under the Convention, countries agreed to limit, reduce, and prevent all types of air pollution, as well as to exchange information, consult, and undertake research. The Convention has been updated with eight specific protocols, two

CONTRIBUTIONS TO GLOBAL WARMING THROUGHOUT THE WORLD

Areas are proportional to historic carbon dioxide emissions from fossil fuel combustion, 1900–1999.

CANADA
2.3%

UNITED STATES
30.3%

EUROPE
27.7%

SOUTH AND
CENTRAL AMERICA
3.8%

Source: World Resources Institute, "Contributions to Global Warming: 1990–1999." www.wri.org.

FORMER SOVIET UNION
13.7%

MIDDLE EAST
2.6%

JAPAN
3.7%

CHINA, INDIA, AND
DEVELOPING ASIA
12.2%

AFRICA
2.5%

AUSTRALIA
1.1%

Industrialized

Developing

of which—the Helsinki and Oslo protocols—deal specifically with SO$_2$ reductions. The Geneva Convention on Long-Range Transboundary Air Pollution was the first legally binding instrument to recognize that air pollution was an international problem.

"Air contamination does not stop at neatly defined regional boundaries."

The Clean Air Act

Around the same time as Europe was realizing that air pollution was an international problem, policy makers in the United States were recognizing that it was more of a national concern than a state or regional concern. The first air pollution control law in the United States—the Air Pollution Control Act of 1955—identified air pollution as a national problem, but the law did not seek to reduce air emissions, only to use national resources to research it. In the next decade, Congress enacted the Clean Air Act of 1963 and the Air Quality Act of 1967. These laws did seek to reduce air emissions, although as laws they were largely seen as inadequate. One of the major flaws identified in the laws, particularly the 1967 Air Quality Act, was the focus on state or regional pollution control, rather than national-level control. "Some of us involved in the enactment of the 1967 statute had significant doubts as to the viability of the regional approach to air pollution control; after all, air contamination does not stop at neatly defined regional boundaries," wrote former U.S. Congressman Paul Rogers in 1990. In 1970, the U.S. Congress sought to rectify the flaws in the 1967 Air Quality Act when it enacted the Clean Air Act of 1970. The 1970 statutes established national, rather than regional, air pollution standards for several air pollutants. According to Rogers, "a national approach to air pollution control remains the only practical way to respond to this problem."[3] The

More than 75 percent of rain in China's Guangdong province is acid rain. A number of international conferences and meetings have been undertaken to address the problems of acid rain, ozone depletion and other environmental threats. AP Images.

1970 Clean Air Act signaled the beginning of national efforts to respond to air pollution.

In the Geneva Convention on Long-Range Transboundary Air Pollution and the 1970 Clean Air Act, policy makers recognized that air pollution transcended regional and geopolitical boundaries. These legal instruments helped pave the way for governments to work together to respond to climate change. One of the most talked-about strategies for addressing climate change is a market-based approach introduced by U.S. policy makers in 1990.

The Concept of Cap and Trade

In 1990, the U.S. Congress and President George H.W. Bush created a new and innovative program to control acid rain. The 1990 Clean Air Act amendments (amendments to the 1970 law) created several new programs to control air pollution. One of these new programs was a "cap-and-trade" program with a goal of cutting SO_2 emissions in half by 2010. The cap-and-trade concept was developed in the late 1960s by economists Ellison Burton and William Sanjour, who worked for the U.S. National Air Pollution Control Administration (predecessor of the Environmental Protection Agency). Burton and Sanjour were comparing the costs of various pollution control strategies. They found that turning the permission to pollute into a commodity, which could be bought and sold, was one of the least costly ways to reduce air pollution. Under the cap-and-trade concept, a government or central authority sets an overall cap on the emissions of a particular air pollutant. The government then allocates permits, which represent the right to emit a specific amount of the air pollutant, to various companies. The companies can then trade the permits among one another in a newly created market, sort of like the stock market. Cap and trade is said to be cost effective because it does not tell companies how to reduce their emissions, but lets them find the best, and presumably cheapest, way to do so. In 1990, when the Acid Rain Program (ARP) was created, its market approach was called "daring" by many people.[4] Soon, it was hailed as one of the most successful pollution control programs ever created. Joel Kurtzman, senior fellow at the nonpartisan Milken Institute, describes the success of the ARP:

> In 2007, three years ahead of schedule, the agency's cap-and-trade program achieved its reduction targets. The cost to emitters, which the Congressional Budget Office had estimated would be $6 billion a year, came instead to about $1.1–$1.8 billion a year, largely because the program enabled emitters to choose their own solutions to the problem, rather than relying on a narrow range of mandated technologies and approaches.[5]

The innovative cap-and-trade program was a demonstrated success.

The Montreal Protocol

When international leaders began trying to devise methods to confront climate change, it was natural for them to look at already-established and successful environmental programs, like the ARP and the Montreal Protocol on Substances That Deplete the Ozone Layer. The Montreal Protocol to protect the ozone layer has been called the "world's most successful environmental treaty"[6] by many including presidents, diplomats, the Environmental Protection Agency, and the United Nations.

The topic of the ozone layer had galvanized the international community during the 1970s and 1980s. Early in the 1970s, two researchers at the University of California, F. Sherwood Rowland and Mario Molina, discovered that substances commonly used as coolants, called chlorofluorocarbons, or CFCs, could destroy the stratospheric ozone layer. A thinner ozone layer would allow greater concentrations of harmful ultraviolet-B radiation to reach the earth's surface. This could cause more skin cancers, eye cataracts, lower yields in agriculture and fisheries, and an increase in ground-level ozone which causes many respiratory problems. In a demonstration of international cooperation, representatives of twenty-four of the world's governments, including the United States, Russia, Japan, and the countries of the European Union came together in Montreal to try to stave off the harmful consequences that would result from a depletion of the ozone layer.

The Montreal Protocol on Substances That Deplete the Ozone Layer (called a protocol because it is an update of a previous treaty—the Vienna Convention for the Protection of the Ozone Layer) was signed on September 16, 1987. The protocol sets out a mandatory timetable for the phaseout of ozone depleting substances. The timetable, which differs for developed nations versus developing ones, is under constant revision, with phaseout dates accelerated in accordance with scientific understanding and technological advances.

The Montreal Protocol is considered a success because it was ratified by every country in the world, most of them soon after

President Reagan Urges the Senate to Ratify the Montreal Protocol

THE WHITE HOUSE
Office of the Press Secretary
For Immediate Release
December 21, 1987

To the Senate of the United States:

I transmit herewith, for the advice and consent of the Senate to ratification, the Montreal Protocol on Substances that Deplete the Ozone Layer, done at Montreal on September 16, 1987. The report of the Department of State is also enclosed for the information of the Senate.

The Montreal Protocol provides for internationally coordinated control of ozone-depleting substances in order to protect public health and the environment from potential adverse effects of depletion of stratospheric ozone. The Protocol was negotiated under the auspices of the United Nations Environment Program, pursuant to the Vienna Convention for the Protection of the Ozone Layer, which was ratified by the United States in August 1986.

In this historic agreement, the international community undertakes cooperative measures to protect a vital global resource. The United States played a leading role in the negotiation of the Protocol. United States ratification is necessary for entry into force and effective implementation of the Protocol. Early ratification by the United States will encourage similar action by other nations whose participation is also essential.

I recommend that the Senate give early and favorable consideration to the Protocol and give its advice and consent to ratification.

Ronald Reagan
The White House
December 21, 1987

SOURCE: Ronald Reagan, "President Reagan on Montreal Protocol Ratification," December 21, 1987.

signing, and because countries actually implemented the agreed-to emissions reductions. Commemorating the seventeenth anniversary of the protocol on September 16, 2004, Kofi Annan, United Nations secretary-general, had these remarks:

> When the Montreal Protocol on Substances That Deplete the Ozone Layer was signed in Montreal 17 years ago, it was not at all clear that it would be possible to phase out ozone-depleting substances within the short period envisaged by the agreement. Today, more than 90 per cent of the global production and consumption of those substances has indeed been phased out. Moreover, consistent progress is being made towards reducing and eliminating any remaining production and consumption. I congratulate all parties to the Montreal Protocol for this remarkable success.[7]

On September 16, 2009, the Montreal Protocol achieved universal participation by all of the world's 196 countries when the young Pacific nation of Timor-Leste ratified it. When announcing his country's ratification of the protocol, Prime Minister Xanana Gusmao said, "Timor-Leste is very pleased to be joining the rest of the world in the fight against the depletion of the ozone layer and the effort towards its recovery. We are proud to be part of this important process to protect the ozone layer and undertake to implement and comply with the Montreal Protocol like all other states that preceded us in this important journey."[8] In the book *Environment and Statecraft*, Scott Barrett tries to understand why the Montreal Protocol was so successful in getting individual countries to reduce their CFC emissions, sometimes to their own detriment. As he notes, "For though every country would benefit from the protection of the ozone layer, each would benefit *whether it contributed to the protection effort or not*, and substituting away from CFCs would be costly. In the jargon of economics, ozone layer protection is a global public good."[9]

Like ozone depletion, actions to address global warming also require individual governments to act for the global public good. Despite the differences between Alaska and the Amazon Rain Forest, the climate is global. Actions in one region of the world can have implications for other regions of the world. As the United States government and governments around the globe seek to address global warming, the models of the Geneva Convention on Long-Range Transboundary Air Pollution, the U.S. Clean Air Act and Acid Rain Program, and the Montreal Protocol are being used to help shape the government's response to global warming.

Notes

1. Paul Krugman, Robin Wells, and Martha Olney, *Essentials of Economics*, New York: Worth Publishers, 2007, p. 259.
2. Quoted in Scott Barrett, *Environment and Statecraft*, New York: Oxford University Press, 2003, p. 7.
3. Paul Rogers, "Looking Back; Looking Ahead: The Clean Air Act of 1990," *EPA Journal*, January-February 1990.
4. Tom Wicker, "Bush's Acid Test," *New York Times*, October 31, 1989.
5. Joel Kurtzman, "The Low-Carbon Diet: How the Market Can Curb Climate Change," *Foreign Affairs*, August 25, 2009.
6. U.S. Environmental Protection Agency, "Montreal Protocol Backgrounder," September 16, 2007. www.epa.gov.
7. "United Nations Secretary-General Says Success of Montreal Protocol Protecting Ozone Layer Should Inspire Parties to Other Environmental Agreements," news release, September 10, 2004. www.unis.unvienna.org.
8. Quoted in United Nations Environment Program, "Ozone Treaty Anniversary Gifts Big Birthday Present to Human Health and Combating of Climate Change," news release, September 16, 2009. www.unep.fr.
9. Barrett, *Environment and Statecraft*, p. 1.

CHAPTER 2

International Recognition of Climate Change

Beginning in the middle of the twentieth century, world leaders started noticing issues related to the climate. Shortly thereafter, many organizations were formed to study and track the climate. These organizations helped to alert the attention of the world and its leaders to the problem of climate change. The international community responded and negotiated a climate change treaty.

The climate first became important to world leaders during World War II. The United States and its allies used weather information to schedule the Normandy invasion and catch the Germans off guard. The date of June 6, 1944, was chosen for D-Day based on predictions that weather over the Normandy coast would be calm that day. At the historic Potsdam Meeting in 1945, U.S. President Harry Truman asked Soviet leader Joseph Stalin to allow U.S. personnel to have access to Soviet weather stations near Japan. The United States was still battling Japan, and U.S. military leaders thought the weather data could prove useful.

After World War II, the United Nations was formed to prevent wars and promote dialogue among the world's nations. In 1950, the World Meteorological Organization (WMO), a one-hundred-year-old weather monitoring group, became the United Nations' authoritative voice on climate. Becoming an agency of the United Nations brought the WMO international authority and stature and provided a platform for geophysical and climate scientists throughout the world to share information.

International Organizations Advance Climate Knowledge

Another important organization was also founded in the 1950s. The International Geophysical Year (IGY) of 1957–1958 was formed to promote international scientific collaboration and cooperation. According to a U.S. National Academy of Sciences report, the IGY was founded "to observe geophysical phenomena and to secure data from all parts of the world; to conduct this effort on a coordinated basis by fields, and in space and time, so that results could be collated in a meaningful manner."[1] The IGY was overseen by an independent federation of international scientific unions, and it received substantial funding from both the United States and the Soviet Union. Much of the money was used to fund research related to the emerging space programs of the two countries. Some money was also afforded to research the

William Reilly (center), head of the U.S. Environmental Protection Agency, answers reporters' questions during a visit to the 1992 Earth Summit. About ten thousand representatives of nongovernmental organizations held a conference parallel to the U.N.-sponsored event. Antonio Scorza/AFP/Getty Images.

topic of climate change, however. In particular, IGY funds were used by American scientists Roger Revelle and Hans Suess (a German émigré) to hire another American scientist by the name of Charles Keeling. It was Keeling's task to gather worldwide data on atmospheric carbon dioxide (CO_2) levels, the key gaseous culprit in the greenhouse effect, which refers to the trapping of heat and warming of the earth by gases in the atmosphere. In 1958, Keeling began measuring atmospheric CO_2 over Antarctica and Hawaii. With his first set of published results in 1960, Keeling became the first person to confirm the rise of atmospheric CO_2 by very precise measurements. The Keeling Curve, as his data has become known, showed that CO_2 released from the burning of fossil fuels and other industrial activities was accumulating in the atmosphere.[2]

During the 1960s and 1970s many important climate organizations were formed, and new scientific techniques were developed that helped advance climate knowledge. The Global Atmospheric Research Program was established by the WMO and the International Council of Scientific Unions. The United States established the National Oceanic and Atmospheric Administration (NOAA) in 1970 and named Robert M. White, chief of the U.S. Weather Bureau, as its chairman. Sophisticated techniques were developed using the carbon-14 isotope (a radioactive form of carbon that forms the basis of the radiocarbon dating method), which allowed scientists to precisely track the movement of carbon in the atmosphere, the oceans, and within living ecosystems.

Gradually, more and more climate change warnings began to be voiced. In 1965, U.S. President Lyndon B. Johnson convened a President's Science Advisory Committee and asked them to report on the problems of environmental pollution. After studying the available data on climate change, including the Keeling Curve, the Environmental Pollution Panel of the committee warned that increasing CO_2 might "modify the heat balance of the atmosphere to such an extent that marked changes in climate, not controllable through local or even national efforts, could occur."[3]

Still, during this time, many scientists either were not concerned about global warming—the common thought was that the earth's oceans and vegetation would absorb the extra CO_2—or they did not think it was an immediate concern because its implications would occur far into the future. Some scientists even thought the earth might be going through a cooling period in the 1970s. This idea was not widely adopted by the larger scientific community, however.

"We must put climate alongside such global commons as the deep seabed and outer space as a concern of mankind for which new international obligations must be derived."

By the mid 1970s, a substantial number of prestigious scientists believed that global warming was occuring and that its impacts could alter the global ecosystem and all of humanity. They began calling on the United Nations and the international governmental community to take action to reduce atmospheric CO_2.

The First Meetings to Confront Climate Change

The first international meeting about global warming, the World Climate Conference, was held in February 1979. The meeting was organized by the WMO and was attended by hundreds of scientists from fifty countries. American meteorologist Robert M. White, chief of the U.S. Weather Bureau and the first administrator of NOAA, was the chairman of the conference. In his keynote address, White said that one of the reasons for the meeting was a "growing appreciation that not only is humanity vulnerable to variations in climate, but climate is also vulnerable to the acts of humanity."[4] White introduced the concept that the climate was a "resource," like water or forests, and furthermore that it was a global resource that needed global protection. In his closing remarks, White said, "For certain purposes we must put climate alongside such global commons as the deep seabed and outer space as a concern of mankind for which new international obligations must be derived."[5] Despite White's comments, most participants at the first World Climate Conference felt that more research was needed before they could ask the world's governments to begin to do something about global warming.

In the years after the first climate conference many scientists and diplomats called for more research and for an international treaty on climate change. British diplomat Crispin Tickell was an active participant in both regards. In the second edition of his book *Climatic Change and World Affairs*, published in 1986, Tickell acknowledged that more scientific information about global warming was needed. Said Tickell, "nearly everyone who has worked on climatic problems begins and ends by bewailing the lack of firm scientific information about them. It is almost a convention that books, reports, and articles on the subject conclude with recommendations for yet further study, yet wider observations, and yet better coordinated action." Tickell said his book was no exception.[6]

Nevertheless, Tickell believed that the evidence that was on hand was compelling enough for governments to act. In *Climatic Change and World Affairs*, Tickell writes that governments of the world should come together and take action on three issues. First, governments should agree on a standard way to cope with climate change, and they should set rules to prevent one country from deleteriously altering the climate and causing damage to other countries. Second, there should be an international prohibition on the use of climate modifications for the purposes of war. Third, governments should work together to facilitate scientific research into climate change.[7]

Appeals for a global treaty were helped along by the popular news media. In his 1989 book, *Global Warming: Are We Enter-*

Science and Politics: The Intergovernmental Panel on Climate Change (IPCC)

The Intergovernmental Panel on Climate Change (IPCC) has been at the center of international climate change policy, and politics, since it was created in 1988. The IPCC was created by the World Meteorological Organization (WMO) and by the United Nations Environment Program (UNEP) in order to help government leaders around the world make informed, science-based decisions about climate change. The IPCC reviews published research from scientists worldwide and produces reports assessing the scientific basis of climate change. One of the primary jobs of the IPCC is to sift through scientific data from many sources and indicate areas where scientists are in consensus, that is, where they agree on the data, where they do not agree, and where there is uncertainty.

The IPCC's first assessment report, issued in 1990, provided a basis for the United Nations Framework Convention on Climate Change treaty. The report indicated that certain emissions resulting from human activities were substantially increasing the atmospheric concentrations of greenhouse gases and causing an increase in the average temperature of the earth. The fourth IPCC assessment report, which was issued

ing the Greenhouse Century, Stanford biology professor Stephen Schneider writes, "In 1988 the environment was as big a story as politics, AIDS, or baseball. Heat, drought, air pollution, and forest fires filled the front pages of newspapers, newsweeklies, and TV news cover stories for months. The greenhouse effect and global warming had emerged from academia and government offices to mingle with popular culture."[8]

With the climate a common news topic and many government officials and academics banging the drum about climate change, the world's leaders met again in a conference similar to the first

in 2007, indicates that there is more scientific certainty for climate change. This report states that "warming of the climate system is unequivocal" and "most of the observed increase in global average temperatures since the mid-twentieth century is very likely due to the observed increase in anthropogenic, i.e. human-caused, greenhouse gas concentrations."

Generally, beginning with the second assessment report (1995), each of the IPCC reports has been criticized as being political. For instance, in 2001, Richard Lindzen, a professor at the Massachusetts Institute for Technology, asserted that the IPCC was politically driven and that scientists were not in agreement about climate change. In an article published by the conservative Heartland Institute, Lindzen writes, "The aura of certainty with which the IPCC's conclusions are being reported is clearly more a matter of politics than science."

The IPCC's fourth assessment report has received criticism from groups claiming it is alarmist, and from groups saying it does not go far enough in stating the dangers of climate change. For instance, University of California climate scientist James Hansen has criticized the report for underestimating the extent of sea-level rise.

Despite the criticisms, the IPCC has been praised. In December 2007, the IPCC was awarded the 2007 Nobel Peace Prize "for their efforts to build up and disseminate greater knowledge about man-made climate change, and to lay the foundations for the measures that are needed to counteract such change."

World Climate Conference but much larger. The United Nations Conference on Environment and Development (UNCED), informally known as the Earth Summit, was held in Rio de Janeiro in June 1992. The Earth Summit attracted 172 government participants, more than three times the number who had attended the first World Climate Conference, and 108 of these countries sent their head of state or government. British prime minister John Major, German chancellor Helmut Kohl, Japanese prime minister Kiichi Miyazawa, and U.S. president George H.W. Bush were all there. Hundreds of native leaders were there as well, including American Indians, Malaysian tribesmen, and Australian Aborigines. Amid all the diplomats and government leaders were nearly ten thousand journalists covering the summit and transmitting its news to hundreds of millions of people around the world.

One of the most important occurrences at the Earth Summit was the signing of the first international treaty on climate change called the United Nations Framework Convention on Climate Change, or UNFCCC. More than 150 nations signed the treaty in Rio de Janeiro and agreed to the "stabilization of greenhouse gas emissions in the atmosphere at a level that would prevent dangerous anthropogenic, i.e. human, interference with the climate system." Furthermore, the nations agreed that such stabilization "should occur in a time-frame sufficient to allow ecosystems to adapt naturally to climate change, to ensure that food production is not threatened and to enable economic development to proceed in a sustainable manner."[9]

In addition to climate change, many other social and environmental issues were discussed at the summit, including biodiversity, population growth, water scarcity, and poverty. In his closing remarks, Canadian environmentalist and secretary general of the summit Maurice Strong addressed UN leaders and commented on the importance of the summit, "The world, Mr. President, will not be the same after this Conference. And the prospects for our Earth cannot, must not, be the same."[10] Strong also commented on the UNFCCC, saying:

> We have taken an historic first step, but only a first step—not a sufficient step. Stabilizing the gaseous composition of the atmosphere is clearly the most urgent problem we will face in the 1990s. Yet the agreement signed here sets neither targets nor timetables. You must now act quickly to bring the climate convention and its protocols in line with what scientists are telling us—that carbon emissions must be cut by at least 60 percent just to put the global warming trend on hold. It is too late for protracted discussions and delay.[11]

In the years following the Rio de Janeiro Earth Summit, several more nations signed and ratified the UNFCCC. Ratification occurs when a signing country officially sanctions the treaty. In the United States, the U.S. Senate must approve a treaty in order for it to become effective. The U.S. Senate approved the UNFCCC, and thus ratified it, in October 1992.

The UNFCCC is not very well known, but without it the more well-known international greenhouse gas reduction agreement, the Kyoto Protocol, would never have been drafted. The UNFCCC's goals of stabilizing greenhouse gas emissions carried with it no penalties for nations that did not meet its objectives. However, the UNFCCC required that the nations signing it meet annually—at Conferences of the Parties, or COPs—to discuss legally binding and enforceable updates (called protocols) to the treaty. In December 1997, the third COP (COP3) took place in Kyoto, Japan, and from it came the Kyoto Protocol, the most well-known climate change agreement. The Kyoto Protocol contains legally binding measures and is more powerful than the UNFCCC.

The Kyoto Protocol

The major feature of the Kyoto Protocol is that it sets binding (i.e., legally enforceable) limits on greenhouse gas emissions—primarily CO_2—from industrialized countries, known as Annex I countries. Under the protocol, each Annex I country agrees to reduce its emissions by a specific percent below the level of greenhouse gases the country emitted in 1990. The twenty-seven members of the European Union, including France, Germany, and the United Kingdom, agreed to cut emissions by 8 percent, Japan by 6 percent, and the United States by 7 percent, below 1990 levels. On average the targets amount to 5 percent less carbon dioxide being emitted into the air globally when compared to 1990 levels. The protocol gives countries from 2008 until 2012 to meet the limits.

Countries can meet the targets in the Kyoto Protocol in a number of ways. They can reduce their emissions of greenhouse

PROGRESS TOWARD MEETING 2012 KYOTO PROTOCOL EMISSIONS TARGETS

2006 figures

On target

Not on target

Incomplete data

EUROPE

Source: "World Ahead of Kyoto Emissions Targets," New Scientist, November 19, 2008. www.newscientist.com.

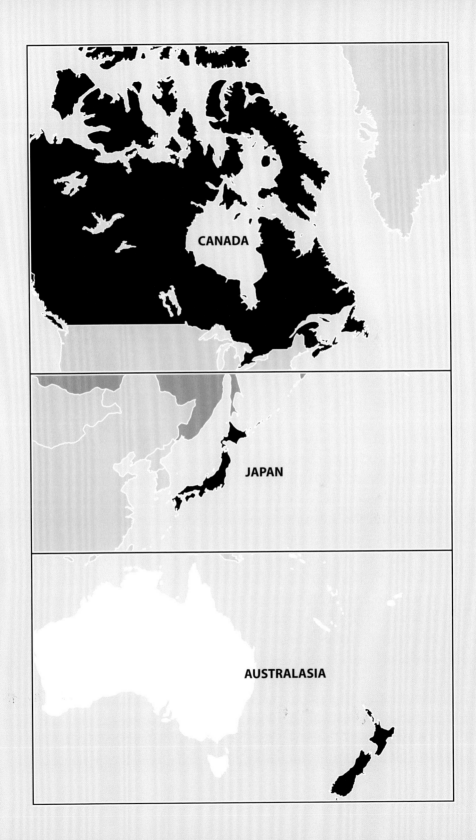

gases, or they can plant trees and do other things to soak up carbon dioxide and help remove it from the atmosphere. Industrialized countries can also get credit toward meeting the protocol's targets by helping developing countries lower their emissions. Under the principle of "common but differentiated responsibilities," which recognizes that developing countries have not contributed to global warming as much as industrialized countries, developing countries, including China and India, are not obligated to reduce their emissions under the protocol. The U.S. government has objected to this particular provision of the Kyoto Protocol.

The United States signed the protocol on November 12, 1998, but President Bill Clinton's administration did not submit the protocol to the Senate for approval. Clinton was concerned that India and China, two large and growing economies, did not have to reduce their greenhouse gas emissions under the protocol. According to the Clinton administration, "The President will not submit the Protocol to the U.S. Senate for approval without the meaningful participation of key developing countries in efforts to address climate change."[12] Soon after George W. Bush took office in January 2001, he issued a statement flatly rejecting the Kyoto Protocol based on the same reasoning used by the Clinton administration. Bush also stated that the protocol could have potentially significant repercussions for the U.S. economy.

Many people were concerned that the U.S. rejection could be a death knell for the treaty. Before the Kyoto Protocol could legally come into force it had to meet two conditions. First, it had to be ratified by at least fifty-five countries. Second, it had to be ratified by countries whose combined greenhouse gas emissions represented at least 55 percent of global emissions. Because the United States is one of the leading greenhouse gas emitters, many people felt its ratification to be crucial. Speaking to the graduating class at Tufts University in May 2001, then U.N. secretary-general Kofi Annan stated, "Today we face the very real danger that the hard-won global gains in combating climate change will experience a grievous setback. The United States, as you probably know, is the world's leading emitter of greenhouse gases, largely because it is the world's most successful economy. That makes . . . especially important [its joining] in reducing emissions and in the broader quest for energy efficiency and conservation."[13]

Despite the U.S. refusal to ratify the treaty, the Kyoto Protocol came into legal force on February 16, 2005, more than seven years after the Kyoto meeting. The first of the two conditions required for the treaty to enter into force was met on May 23, 2002, when Iceland became the fifty-fifth country to ratify the Protocol. When Russia ratified the agreement in November 2004, the second condition was satisfied—the combined emissions of all ratifying countries represented at least 55 percent of global emissions. Ninety days after Russia's ratification, the Kyoto Protocol entered into force.

Beyond the Kyoto Protocol

Although there have been many international climate change meetings since 1997, almost one decade into the twenty-first century the Kyoto Protocol is still the most recognizable international climate change agreement.

Many people had hoped that COP15, which took place in Copenhagen, Denmark, in December 2009, would provide a treaty that stipulated national greenhouse gas reductions after Kyoto expires in 2012. Copenhagen fell short of expectations, however. Virtually every nation—193 countries—participated in the Copenhagen climate talks. However, the agreement that came out of meetings—the Copenhagen Accord—was drafted late on the last night of the conference by Barack Obama of the United States, Nicolas Sarkozy of France, Angela Merkel of Germany, Gordon Brown of the United Kingdom, Felipe Calderón of Mexico, and twenty other national leaders. The accord was not formally adopted as the official outcome of Copenhagen because of protests by some of the nations left out of the final negotiations. World leaders did agree to take note of the Copenhagen Accord, however.

In the Copenhagen Accord, countries did not agree to specific, legally binding greenhouse gas reductions, as many had hoped. Instead, each country promised to reduce its own emissions in order to limit the global temperature increase to no more than 3.6°F (2°C), the threshold identified by scientists as being critical to avoiding some of the worst climate change scenarios. Industrialized countries pledged to set emission reduction targets and begin reaching them by 2020. Developing countries also pledged to voluntarily reduce emissions. Because pledges listed by developed and developing countries may not be enough to keep global temperature rise below the targeted amount, leaders called for a review of the accord to be completed by 2015.

The Copenhagen Accord may signal a shift in how the world addresses climate change. In the weeks after the talks, many people discussed the significance of the world's leaders' failure to adopt a legally binding treaty. Writing in the *New Republic* in February 2010, assistant editor Bradford Plumer observes that, "the Copenhagen framework moves away from the old notion of a global treaty with legally binding targets. Instead, under the current Copenhagen Accord, countries are voluntarily setting their own national targets." Plumer notes that this may be a more realistic approach, as "plenty of countries had obligations to cut emissions under the Kyoto Protocol, but they never actually followed through."[14]

Speaking to reporters after the Copenhagen conference, U.S. president Barack Obama called it a "meaningful" beginning to a new global consensus toward limiting greenhouse gas emissions. He also acknowledged that COP15 failed to produce a "legally binding" pact, however, and doing so anytime soon would be "very hard."[15]

Notes

1. National Academy of Sciences, "The International Geophysical Year," 2005. www.nationalacademies.org.

2. Spencer Weart, "The Discovery of Global Warming: The Carbon Dioxide Greenhouse Effect," American Institute of Physics, 2008. www.aip.org.

3. Thomas Peterson, William M. Connolley, and John Fleck, "The Myth of the 1970s Global Cooling Scientific Consensus," *Bulletin of the American Meteorological Society*, September 2008.

4. Robert White, "Climate at the Millennium," *Environment*, April 1979, pp. 31–32.

5. White, "Climate at the Millennium," pp. 31–32.

6. Crispin Tickell, *Climatic Change and World Affairs*, 2nd Edition, Lanham, MD: University Press of America, 1986, Ch. 3.

7. Tickell, *Climatic Change and World Affairs*, Ch. 3.

8. Stephen Schneider, *Global Warming: Are We Entering the Greenhouse Century?* San Francisco: Sierra Club Books, 1989, Preface.

9. United Nations, "United Nations Framework Convention on Climate Change," 1992. http://unfccc.int.

10. Maurice Strong, "Closing Statement to the Rio Summit," MauriceStrong.net, June 14, 1992. www.mauricestrong.net.

11. Strong, "Closing Statement to the Rio Summit."

12. "The U.S. View: Fact Sheet on the Kyoto Protocol." http://clinton5.nara.gov/media/pdf/3bonkyoto.pdf.

13. Kofi Annan, "Address by Kofi Annan at the Fletcher School of Law and Diplomacy Tufts University," United Nations, May 21, 2001. www.un.org.

14. Bradford Plumer, "Copenhagen Deadline Comes and Goes. Now What?" *New Republic*, February 1, 2010. www.tnr.com.

15. Major Garrett, "Copenhagen Climate Conference Ends with Whimper, No Legally Binding Pact, No Commitment to Pursue One in 2010," *Fox News*, December 18, 2009. http://whitehouse.blogs.foxnews.com.

CHAPTER 3

Historical U.S. Response to Climate Change

The U.S. government has studied, discussed, and reported on climate change for several decades. Most U.S. government plans to address climate change have involved convincing companies and businesses to voluntarily reduce carbon dioxide (CO_2) emissions. Federal plans have generally stopped short of requiring mandatory emission reductions over concerns that doing so will hurt the U.S. economy. In the absence of federal regulation, several states have addressed climate change on their own or as members of regional initiatives.

Early Government Reports Address Global Warming

Many people mark the first moment that the highest levels of the U.S. government got involved in climate change as occurring in 1979, when the Council on Environmental Quality submitted a report to President Jimmy Carter. The report, titled *The Carbon Dioxide Problem*, was authored by four eminent American scientists: George Woodwell, Gordon MacDonald, Roger Revelle, and David Keeling. It begins with this sentence: "Man is setting in motion a series of events that seem certain to cause a significant warming of world climates over the next decades unless mitigating steps are taken immediately."[1] Carter read the report and submitted it to the Department of Energy (DOE). The agency did not react favorably to the report, as abiding by its premise would undermine a massive DOE program promoting the use of synthetic liquid fuels made from coal and oil shale. Nevertheless, Carter asked the National Academy of Sciences to study the issue. That body's report, also released in 1979, was no less worrying. National Academy of Sciences Climate Research Board chairman Verner Suomi's summary states: "The conclusions of this brief but intense investigation may be comforting to scientists but disturbing to policymakers. If CO_2 continues to increase, the study group finds no reason to doubt that climate changes will result and no reason to believe that these changes will be negligible. A wait-and-see policy may mean waiting until it is too late."[2] Suomi did point out, however, that the ocean—he referred to it as "the great and ponderous flywheel of the global climate system"—may be expected to slow the course of climate change.[3]

During the 1980s, many more government bodies discussed, studied, and issued reports about climate change. The first of many Environmental Protection Agency (EPA) reports was issued in 1983. The report, titled *Can We Delay a Greenhouse Warming?*, concluded that the evidence of global warming continues to accumulate, but considerable uncertainty exists regarding its impact. In the report the EPA also acknowledges various pools of thought on how to address climate change, stating:

> Responses to the threat of a greenhouse warming are polarized. Many have dismissed it as too speculative or too distant to be of concern. Some assume that technological options will emerge to prevent a warming, or, at worst, to ameliorate harmful consequences. Others argue that only an immediate and radical change in the rate of CO_2 emissions can avert worldwide catastrophe. The risks are high in pursuing a "wait and see" attitude on one hand, or in acting impulsively on the other.[4]

U.S. Congress Hears About Climate Change

By the middle of the 1980s, members of the U.S. Congress such as senators David Durenberger from Minnesota, Al Gore from

Tennessee, and John Chafee from Rhode Island began focusing on the issue. Chafee's congressional hearings were particularly noteworthy. They would mark the first time that members of Congress called on the executive branch to determine what could be done about climate change. Additionally, climate change was discussed in conjunction with ozone depletion, which at the time

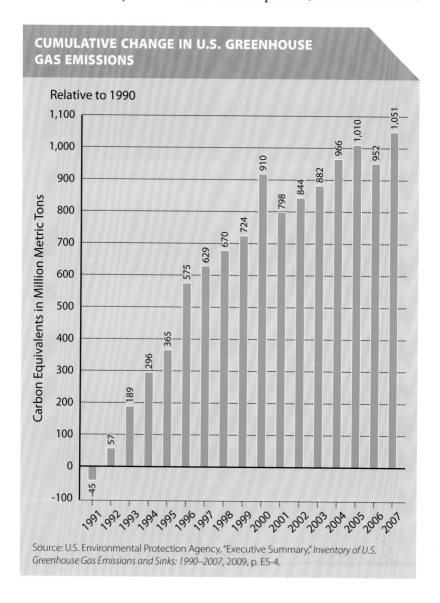

CUMULATIVE CHANGE IN U.S. GREENHOUSE GAS EMISSIONS

Relative to 1990

Source: U.S. Environmental Protection Agency, "Executive Summary," *Inventory of U.S. Greenhouse Gas Emissions and Sinks: 1990–2007*, 2009, p. ES-4.

was a bigger public issue. As a result the hearings garnered extra media attention for climate change. After the hearings, Congress appropriated funds to study climate change.

By the end of the 1980s, some of the first policy recommendations to address climate change were made, and the first climate change law was enacted. In 1987, the Senate Environment and Public Works Committee heard testimony from scientists about climate change. V. Ramanathan from the National Center for Atmospheric Research testified that "it was no longer a question of whether climate change would occur, but when."[5] Geochemist Wally Broecker testified that a buildup of greenhouse gases "could force the climate system into rapid and unpredictable change."[6] During a Senate Energy Committee hearing on climate change, Gordon MacDonald, one of the authors of the 1979 Council on Environmental Quality report, suggested that consideration be given to a carbon tax to discourage the use of carbon dioxide–emitting fossil fuels. In 1988, President Ronald Reagan signed a law that included an amendment called the Global Climate Protection Act. That act called on the president and the EPA to begin to develop a strategy to respond to climate change.

As the 1980s turned into the 1990s, it became apparent that despite all the warnings and dire predictions about climate change, there were a substantial number of climate change skeptics. President George H.W. Bush's White House chief of staff, John Sununu, was one such skeptic. He felt that the scientific evidence for the greenhouse effect was flimsy and that taking action to curb CO_2 emissions would be economically devastating to the country. Although Sununu resigned as chief of staff in December 1991, he made an enduring impression on the first President Bush.

Presidential Plans to Address Greenhouse Gas Emissions

In 1992, President George H.W. Bush argued against an international treaty calling for mandatory greenhouse gas reductions. As the world's leaders negotiated over the language of the U.N.

Framework Convention on Climate Change (UNFCCC), Bush made it clear that the United States would not sign a treaty that obligated itself to reduce greenhouse gas emissions. The U.S. position carried a great deal of weight with the other world leaders, and so the final draft of the UNFCCC called for voluntary, rather than mandatory, CO_2 reductions. The countries that signed and ratified the UNFCCC agreed to try to reduce CO_2 emissions to their 1990 levels by 2000. President Bush signed the treaty at the 1992 Earth Summit in Rio de Janeiro, and the U.S. Senate ratified it later that year.

During the presidency of Bill Clinton, the U.S. government continued to favor voluntary, rather than mandatory, emission reductions. President Clinton's Climate Change Action Plan contained forty-four different steps that would help the country meet the goals of the UNFCC. The plan did not require CO_2 emission reductions, but instead provided incentives for businesses to voluntarily reduce emissions. During this time, the United States took part in meetings to update the UNFCCC, called Conferences of the Parties, held in Berlin in 1995 and Geneva in 1996. The U.S. EPA also began tracking the country's greenhouse gas emissions. Later in the decade, Clinton signed the Kyoto Protocol, which contained mandatory greenhouse gas reductions. Clinton was not happy with the protocol, however, because it did not require binding emission reductions from China, India, and other developing countries. He never submitted the protocol to the Senate for ratification, so the United States was not bound to its emission reductions.

Soon after George W. Bush took office in 2001, he announced that he was officially withdrawing the United States from the Kyoto Protocol because the protocol was not in the country's best interests. Bush's official statement calls the Kyoto Protocol "fundamentally flawed" and says that the goals in the protocol

Following page: The United States has sometimes come under scrutiny for its reaction to world climate change policies, such as when George W. Bush withdrew the United States from the Kyoto Protocol in 2001. Sean Gallup/Getty Images.

were "established not by science, but by political negotiation."[7] Bush said he was going to implement a practical plan to address air pollution and climate change, and in February 2002, he announced the Clear Skies and Global Climate Change initiatives.

Like the presidential plans of Bill Clinton and George H.W. Bush, George W. Bush's plan was based on voluntary CO_2 reductions. The plan called for an 18 percent reduction in emissions intensity—the ratio of emissions to gross domestic product by 2010. This approach took into account the economic growth of the country. Under Bush's plan, the voluntary reductions would largely be achieved by establishing tax credits to support the invention and adoption of energy-saving technologies and promote expanded CO_2 absorption by forestry and agriculture. The Bush administration created the National Climate Change Research Initiative and the National Climate Change Technology Initiative to invest in research and new technologies.

During the 1980s, the 1990s, and the first decade of the twenty-first century, the U.S. government response to climate change was largely unchanging. There were congressional hearings and reports from government agencies, such as the EPA, DOE, National Academy of Sciences, and others. Meanwhile, the government called on American industries to voluntarily reduce CO_2 emissions. At congressional hearings, scientists would issue predictions of climate catastrophe if CO_2 emissions continued unabated. There were always other witnesses testifying that the science behind global warming was too uncertain, however, and that acting to curb CO_2 emissions would be imprudent and have devastating economic implications. Bills were introduced in the U.S. Congress to curb CO_2 and other greenhouse gas emissions, but they were never enacted.

States Develop Regional Initiatives to Reduce Emissions

In the absence of national regulatory action to reduce CO_2 and other greenhouse gas emissions, U.S. states began forming regional greenhouse gas initiatives or acting on their own early in the 2000s. Many states were concerned about the toll climate change would take on their economies, many of which are closely tied to natural resources. Coastal states considered the impact of rising sea levels, agricultural states worried about lost productivity, and the dry western states were alarmed by the prospect of worsening droughts. Many states also looked at policies that addressed climate change as economic opportunities: to produce and sell alternative fuels, to become renewable energy exporters, or to attract high-tech businesses.

An agreement between the governors of northeastern and mid-Atlantic states to reduce CO_2 emissions laid the basis for the first mandatory reduction program in North America. In 2003, the governors of Connecticut, Delaware, Maine, Massachusetts, New Hampshire, New Jersey, New York, Rhode Island, and Vermont began developing the Regional Greenhouse Gas Initiative (RGGI) to reduce CO_2 emissions from power plants. The governors decided that the RGGI would reduce CO_2 by establishing a cap-and-trade program, which is a market-based approach to pollution control that turns the permission to pollute into a commodity that can be bought and sold. Under the RGGI's cap-and-trade approach, each state establishes a steadily declining cap on CO_2 emissions and requires power plants to hold an emission allowance for every ton of CO_2 they emit into the air. The RGGI began implementation in January 2009. The participating states are hoping that under the initiative they can reduce their combined CO_2 emissions to 2002–2004 levels by 2015, and then reduce them by another 10 percent between 2015 and 2020.[8]

In 2007, western and midwestern states devised their own greenhouse gas initiatives. The Western Climate Initiative (WCI) was established in February 2007 by the governors of Arizona, California, New Mexico, Oregon, and Washington. The goal of the WCI is to reduce regional CO_2 and greenhouse gas emissions to 15 percent below 2005 levels by 2020, also using a cap-and-trade approach. The WCI has since been joined by Montana and Utah, as well as the Canadian provinces of British Columbia, Manitoba, Ontario, and Quebec.

The Midwestern Greenhouse Gas Accord, established in November 2007, is also based on a cap-and-trade approach. Six Midwest states—Iowa, Illinois, Kansas, Michigan, Minnesota, and Wisconsin—as well as the Canadian province of Manitoba are members of the accord. The accord aims to develop a market-based cap-and-trade program and reduce CO_2 levels by 20 percent below 2005 levels by 2020.[9]

California Takes Action

California has been the most aggressive of U.S. states in trying to reduce CO_2 emissions. California has the most people and the biggest economy of any state in the nation. Additionally, the state's environmental agency, the California Air Resources Board (CARB), has been around longer than the U.S. EPA. Typically, California is the first state to enact environmental regulations. On July 22, 2002, California governor Gray Davis signed Assembly Bill 1493 into law, requiring CARB to develop what would have been the nation's first greenhouse gas emission standards for automobiles. CARB set about doing its work and, in 2005, requested a waiver from the EPA to allow California to regulate automobile greenhouse gas emissions. Because CARB was in operation before the formation of the EPA, California has the authority to pass stronger air pollution standards than ones set by the federal government, if it can get a waiver from the EPA. Otherwise, states cannot be more stringent than the federal government. Under the administration of George W. Bush, the EPA denied the waiver, stating that "greenhouse gases have national effects in an equal measure regardless of where the emissions occurred," and the agency "advocated a national approach to the greenhouse gas problem."[10] Soon after Barack Obama became president, however, his EPA administrator granted the waiver and opened the door for California to limit the level of CO_2 that is emitted from the tailpipes of automobiles and trucks.

California did not stop with the automobile regulations. In 2007, the state enacted a law called the California Global Warming Solutions Act of 2006. This law was drafted by the same legislator—Fran Pavley—who drafted the 2002 law establishing automobile emissions standards. The Global Warming Solutions Act would bring California into compliance with the Kyoto Protocol by capping California greenhouse gas emissions at 1990 levels by 2020. The law directs CARB to identify the best strategy—whether cap and trade, taxation, or more traditional regulations, such as requiring emitters of CO_2 to hold permits—to meet the 2020 target.

"It is true that for too many years, mankind has been slow to respond to or even recognize the magnitude of the climate threat. It is true of my own country as well. . . . But this is a new day. It is a new era."

National Cap and Trade?

The United States is still writing its historical response to climate change. As 2009 came to a close, two cap-and-trade bills had been offered in the U.S. Congress. Henry Waxman's and Ed Markey's comprehensive American Clean Energy and Security Act includes a portion titled the Safe Climate Act, which establishes a cap-and-trade program for CO_2. It was passed out of the House of Representatives in June 2009. Another bill that would establish a CO_2 cap-and-trade program was introduced by senators Barbara Boxer and John Kerry in the fall of 2009. Both bills have a long way to go before either one can become law. Only once it is in a form agreed upon by both chambers of Congress, that is, the House and the Senate, and receives the president's signature does a piece of legislation become a law. In his first address to the United Nations, in September 2009, President Obama indicated that he supports a CO_2 cap-and-trade program

The Safe Climate Act

TITLE III—REDUCING GLOBAL WARMING POLLUTION
SEC. 301. SHORT TITLE.

This title, and sections 112, 116, 221, 222, 223, and 401 of this Act, and the amendments made by this title and those sections, may be cited as the "Safe Climate Act."

(a) FINDINGS.—The Congress finds as follows:

    (1) Global warming poses a significant threat to the national security, economy, public health and welfare, and environment of the United States, as well as of other nations. . . .

    (6) Nations of the world look to the United States for leadership in addressing the threat of and harm from global warming. Full implementation of the Safe Climate Act is critical to engage other nations in an international effort to mitigate the threat of and harm from global warming.

    (7) Global warming and its adverse effects are occurring and are likely to continue and increase in magnitude, and to do so at a greater and more harmful rate, unless the Safe Climate Act is fully implemented and enforced in an expeditious manner.

(b) PURPOSE.—It is the general purpose of the Safe Climate Act to help prevent, reduce the pace of, mitigate, and remedy global warming and its adverse effects. To fulfill such purpose, it is necessary to—

    (1) require the timely fulfillment of all governmental acts and duties, both substantive and procedural, and the prompt compliance of covered entities with the requirements of the Safe Climate Act;

    (2) establish and maintain an effective, transparent, and fair market for emission allowances and preserve the integrity of the cap on emissions and of offset credits. . . .

SOURCE: **American Clean Energy and Security Act of 2009 [H.R. 2454] (Engrossed as Agreed to or Passed by the House), June 26, 2009.**

and that his administration's plan to deal with climate change will be different than that of his predecessors. President Obama said, "It is true that for too many years, mankind has been slow to respond to or even recognize the magnitude of the climate threat. It is true of my own country as well. . . . But this is a new day. It is a new era."[11]

Notes

1. George M. Woodwell, Gordon J. MacDonald, Roger Revelle, and C. David Keeling, *The Carbon Dioxide Problem: Implications for Policy in the Management of Energy and Other Resources, a Report to the Council on Environmental Quality,* 1979. www.nytimes.com.
2. *Carbon Dioxide and Climate: A Scientific Assessment Report, of an Ad Hoc Study Group on Carbon Dioxide and Climate,* National Research Council, National Academy of Sciences, Washington, DC, 1979.
3. *Carbon Dioxide and Climate,* National Research Council.
4. U.S. Environmental Protection Agency, *Can We Delay a Greenhouse Warming?* Washington, DC, September 1983.
5. Rafe Pomerance, "The Dangers from Climate Warming: A Public Awakening," in *The Challenge of Global Warming,* ed. Dean Abrahamson, Washington DC: Island Press, 1989.
6. Pomerance, "The Dangers from Climate Warming: A Public Awakening."
7. "Fact Sheet: United States Policy on the Kyoto Protocol," Public Affairs Section, U.S. Embassy, Vienna, Austria.
8. Regional Greenhouse Gas Initiative, "RGGI Fact Sheet," April 22, 2009. www.rggi.org.
9. Midwestern Greenhouse Gas Reduction Accord, "Draft Final Recommendations of the Advisory Group," June 2009. www.midwesternaccord.org.
10. U.S. Environmental Protection Agency, "EPA's California Waiver Decision on Greenhouse Gas Automobile Emissions Met Statutory Procedural Requirements," Rep. no. 09-P-0056, December 9, 2008.
11. Barack Obama, "Remarks by the President at United Nations Secretary-General Ban Ki-Moon's Climate Change Summit," WhiteHouse.gov, September 22, 2009. www.whitehouse.gov.

CHAPTER 4

Regulating Carbon Dioxide

Carbon dioxide is the most significant greenhouse gas. There are other gases released into the atmosphere that warm the earth, such as methane, nitrous oxide, and synthetic fluorinated gases. Carbon dioxide emissions dwarf the emissions of these other gases, however, and so have a bigger warming impact on the earth. As a result, government climate change policies focus primarily on reducing carbon dioxide (CO_2) emissions.

The Kyoto Protocol, a landmark international treaty to reduce CO_2 emissions, recognizes six greenhouse gases whose emissions contribute to global warming. The six warming gases are: 1) CO_2, which is emitted from the burning of fossil fuels to power automobiles, create heat and electricity, and drive manufacturing processes; 2) methane (CH_4) and 3) nitrous oxide (N_2O) from agricultural activities and landfills; and synthetic fluorinated gases, such as 4) hydrofluorocarbons (HFCs), 5) perfluorocarbons (PFCs), and 6) sulfur hexafluoride (SF_6), which are used as refrigerants and in the electronics industry. These six greenhouse gases are identified specifically for emissions reductions in the Kyoto Protocol.

Global Warming Potential

Pound for pound, synthetic fluorinated gases are the most potent greenhouse gases. Scientists have devised a unit of measurement called global warming potential, or GWP, to convey the ability of a gas to warm the earth. The GWP of a gas indicates how much heat per unit of weight it can absorb and how long it can stay in the atmosphere. Synthetic gases containing multiple fluorine atoms, such as HFCs, PFCs, and SF_6, are potent heat-trapping gases that can exist in the atmosphere for thousands of years. Therefore, these gases have the highest GWP. For instance, the GWP of SF_6 is 22,800.[1]

CO_2 has a GWP of 1 and is the least potent greenhouse gas. Its emissions dwarf those of the other gases, however, and therefore it has the greatest impact on warming the earth. CO_2 is released into the atmosphere in large quantities on a continual basis. It is estimated that there are 900 million to 1 billion gasoline- and diesel-fueled vehicles in the world, and each one of them emits CO_2 every time it is driven. Whenever heat is generated from natural gas furnaces, or electricity is produced at power plants, CO_2 is emitted. Most industrial and manufacturing processes also release CO_2 into the air. Thus, even though it has a GWP of just 1 and other greenhouse gases are more potent, reducing CO_2 is the focus of most government climate change policies.

CO_2 Differs from Other "Pollutants"

Carbon dioxide is very different from most other air emissions that governments try to control. CO_2 is not *directly* harmful to human health or the environment. CO_2 is a benign, ever-present compound necessary for life. CO_2 is the final product of energy processes that occur in the cells of humans and animals and is expelled in every breath. Volcanoes and decaying vegetation also release CO_2 into the atmosphere. These natural sources of CO_2 constitute part of a natural cycle. Photosynthetic processes, wherein green plants take in CO_2 and release oxygen, make up the other part of the cycle.

In contrast, most air emissions governments regulate are considered pollutants. Gases such as sulfur dioxide, nitrogen oxides, and mercury are regulated by governments because they are harmful to human health and the environment. Sulfur dioxide and nitrogen oxides emitted from power plants cause acid rain, which kills lakes, causes haze, and damages stonework. Mercury emissions deposit in lakes and streams and accumulate in fish and other aquatic animals. Most states issue mercury advisories, warning people about eating fish that may contain mercury.

The Clean Air Act and the Definition of an Air Pollutant

The U.S. Clean Air Act—the country's preeminent air pollution control law—was enacted in 1970 and amended in 1990. The intent of the Clean Air Act is to protect air quality and reduce emissions of air pollutants from power plants, factories, and automobiles. The U.S. Environmental Protection Agency (EPA) is responsible for implementing the act. The agency has effectively dealt with sulfur dioxide, nitrogen oxides, ozone, and other air emissions traditionally known as air pollutants.

Under Section 202 of the Clean Air Act, if the EPA determines an emission from automobiles to be an air pollutant that endangers public health or welfare, the agency is required to regulate the emission of that air pollutant from new motor vehicles. This section of the Clean Air Act and the determination of whether greenhouse gases are air pollutants have become especially important in the reduction of CO_2 emissions.

Whether CO_2 should be considered an air pollutant under the Clean Air Act has been hotly debated for many years. The Clean Air Act defines an air pollutant as "any air pollution agent or combination of such agents, including any physical, chemical, biological, radioactive substance or matter [that is] emitted into or otherwise enters the ambient air."[2] During President George W. Bush's administration, from 2001 to 2008, the EPA held that CO_2 was not an air pollutant because it is a natural component of the atmosphere. Furthermore, the agency contended that the Clean Air Act did not require the agency to address climate change, and even if it did, there was too much scientific uncertainty about the causes and effects of global warming to put

In 2007, the Supreme Court ruled that greenhouse gases such as those emitted by this power plant in El Segundo, California are pollutants and therefore must be regulated by the U.S. Environmental Protection Agency. David McNew/Getty Images.

controls on carbon dioxide. States including California, Illinois, Massachusetts, and New Mexico; the cities of New York and Baltimore; and environmental organizations including Greenpeace, the International Center for Technology Assessment, and the Sierra Club were not satisfied with this conclusion. They believed carbon dioxide's contribution to global warming qualified it as pollutant. These groups took the EPA to court over its decision and the case eventually went to the U.S. Supreme Court.

On April 2, 2007 the Supreme Court issued a decision in the case, called *Massachusetts et al. v. EPA et al.* The Supreme Court ruled, among other things, that CO_2, and greenhouse gases in general, are air pollutants and as such are covered under the Clean Air Act. Justice John Paul Stevens, in delivering the Court's opinion states, "Because greenhouse gases fit well within the Clean Air Act's capacious definition of "air pollutant," we hold that EPA has the statutory authority to regulate the emission of such gases from new motor vehicles."[3] The decision was close: Five justices agreed with Massachusetts and the other plaintiffs, while four justices agreed with the EPA. The justices in dissent felt that carbon dioxide and other greenhouse gases did not necessarily fall within the definition of air pollutant in the Clean Air Act. Speaking for the dissent, Justice Antonin Scalia stated, "Regulating the buildup of CO_2 and other greenhouse gases in the upper reaches of the atmosphere, which is alleged to be causing global climate change, is not akin to regulating the concentration of some substance that is polluting the air."[4]

"The EPA Administrator found that emissions of CO_2 and other greenhouse gases [are] endangering public health and welfare."

After the Supreme Court decision, which validated calling CO_2 an air pollutant, the EPA had to go back and make a determination of a different sort. The agency had to decide whether CO_2 and other greenhouse gases endanger human health and welfare. If the decision is yes, under Section 202 of the Clean Air Act, it is required to regulate CO_2.

Shortly after Barack Obama became president in 2009, and two years after the Supreme Court decision, the EPA made a historic determination. On April 17, 2009, the newly appointed administrator of the EPA, Lisa Jackson, proposed an "endangerment finding." It states that, "the EPA Administrator found that emissions of CO_2 and other greenhouse gases from automobiles are contributing to air pollution, which is endangering public health and welfare under the Clean Air Act."[5]

The Supreme Court decision and the EPA's proposal to determine endangerment are hailed by many as important steps on the road to reducing CO_2 emissions. The question of whether they are enough to pave the way for carbon dioxide regulations in the United States is debatable, however. Business groups and right-leaning organizations maintain that EPA cannot or should

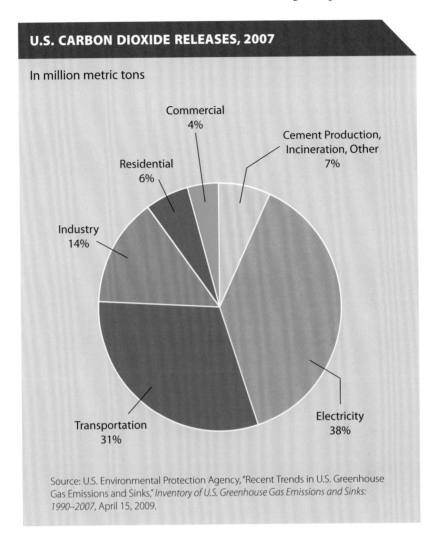

U.S. CARBON DIOXIDE RELEASES, 2007

In million metric tons

Commercial
4%

Cement Production,
Incineration, Other
7%

Residential
6%

Industry
14%

Transportation
31%

Electricity
38%

Source: U.S. Environmental Protection Agency, "Recent Trends in U.S. Greenhouse Gas Emissions and Sinks," *Inventory of U.S. Greenhouse Gas Emissions and Sinks: 1990–2007*, April 15, 2009.

not act to regulate CO_2 without a legislative mandate from the U.S. Congress. They argue that the Clean Air Act is not designed to deal with CO_2. In a letter to the EPA, the U.S. Small Business Association argued that "the current Clean Air Act is neither an effective nor an efficient mechanism for EPA to use to regulate greenhouse gases, regulating carbon dioxide for the first time under the Clean Air Act will be complex and disruptive, and regulating CO_2 and other greenhouse gases under the Clean Air

Act will negatively impact small entities, including small businesses and small communities."[6] Members of the environmental community agree to some extent, contending that it would be best if Congress enacted legislation. However, they also believe that the Supreme Court decision and the EPA's finding of endangerment are, in the words of David Doniger of the Natural Resources Defense Council, "a backup plan."[7] According to Kevin Knobloch, president of the Union of Concerned Scientists, "the potential severity of climate change means we can't afford to wait until Congress enacts legislation and the administration puts it into practice. So while Congress works on a bill, the Environmental Protection Agency should begin right away to regulate global warming pollution under the Clean Air Act."[8]

Congressional Action to Regulate Carbon Dioxide

The U.S. Congress has considered legislation to reduce emissions of CO_2 since the late 1980s. The National Global Warming Policy Act was introduced in the U.S. Senate by Colorado Congressman Tim Wirth in March 1989. The bill set an initial goal of 20-percent reductions on CO_2 emissions from 1988 levels by 2001. Since then, many other members of Congress have also introduced legislation to reduce CO_2 emissions.

Legislators have generally introduced legislation that focuses on incentive-based approaches, rather than command-and-control approaches, to reduce CO_2 emissions. Command-and-control approaches generally give the EPA broad authority to require that businesses reduce air emissions to certain specific levels by installing pollution control equipment. Alternatively, incentive-based policies provide an economic incentive for businesses and consumers to reduce emissions. The main principle of an incentive-based approach to pollution control is that the environmental attributes of a product or commodity, such as electricity, heat, or fuel, are reflected in the price consumers pay. For instance, many people contend that if the costs associated with the environmental impacts of coal, such as mercury contamination of lakes or sulfur dioxide emissions, were fully incorporated into the price of electricity, coal-produced electricity would cost considerably more than it does now. At a March 2009 meeting of the International Scientific Congress on Climate Change held in Copenhagen, Denmark, Yale professor of economics William Nordhaus explained why many policy makers have focused on using economics to devise CO_2 reduction strategies:

> If economics provides a single bottom line for policy, it is that we need to correct this market failure by ensuring that all people, everywhere, and for the indefinite future face a market price for the use of carbon that reflects the social costs of their activities. . . . Economic participants—thousands of governments, millions of firms, billions of people, all making trillions of decisions each year—need to face realistic prices for the use of carbon if their decisions about consumption, investment, and innovation are to be appropriate.[9]

Cap and Trade

The most talked about incentive-based approach to reducing CO_2 emissions is a cap-and-trade program. Cap-and-trade programs are market-based approaches because they turn the permission to pollute into a commodity that can be bought and sold. The idea behind a cap-and-trade program is to put a price on pollution that motivates businesses to find ways to reduce their air pollutant emissions. The federal Acid Rain Program established by the U.S. Congress in 1990 to control emissions of sulfur dioxide is an example of a cap-and-trade program. A basic cap-and-trade program works by:

- Setting a yearly nationwide limit, or *cap* (expressed in tons for CO_2), on emissions of a particular air pollutant. Each year the cap gets smaller and smaller, until an ultimate reduction goal is reached.

- Creating "emission allowances" that give whoever owns them (factories, power plants, etc.) the permission to emit the air pollutant. Each emission allowance gives a business permission to emit one ton of the air pollutant. The total number of emission allowances equals the nationwide cap.
- Distributing emission allowances to businesses. Emission allowances might be auctioned off, and provide revenues to the government, or they could be given freely to businesses, based on their past emissions history.
- Requiring businesses to monitor and report their emissions on a regular basis. They have to show that they own an emission allowance for every ton of air pollutant they emit into the air.
- Creating a market (like the stock market) where businesses may *trade* emission allowances amongst each other. Businesses that are better at reducing pollutant emissions may own more emission allowances than they need. These companies can sell their excess allowances to businesses that have a hard time reducing their emissions. In this way emission allowances acquire a monetary value.

According to the Environmental Defense Fund, an organization that supports a CO_2 cap-and-trade program, "cap and trade harnesses the forces of markets to achieve cost-effective environmental protection. Markets can achieve superior environmental protection by giving businesses both flexibility and a direct financial incentive to find faster, cheaper and more innovative ways to reduce pollution."[10] In addition to reducing greenhouse gas emissions, some proponents of a CO_2 cap-and-trade program also contend it will create jobs by spurring investment in renewable energy and energy efficiency. Economist Paul Krugman made this point in an opinion piece about cap and trade in the May 1, 2009, *New York Times*. Writes Krugman, "a commitment to greenhouse gas reduction would, in the short-to-medium run, have the same economic effects as a major technological innova-

Carbon Offsets Gain in Popularity

Carbon offsets have become all the rage recently: the winter Olympics of 2006 in Turin, Al Gore, the U.S. country-rock trio Dixie Chicks, and Hollywood actor George Clooney all buy offsets in an effort to become "carbon neutral." *The New Oxford American Dictionary* even chose "carbon neutral" as the Word of the Year for 2006. As public awareness of the driving role carbon emissions play in climate change becomes nearly universal, the pressure to take action is increasing and many firms and individuals who have decided they want to do something about it are purchasing offsets. . . .

The concept is very simple. All fossil-fuel powered vehicles (as well as fossil-fired power plants and factories) emit CO_2 during operation. Commercial jets are no exception and collectively contribute a significant share of global annual emissions. So let's say you fly on a commercial carrier from Chicago to Amsterdam. You would use one of the many online carbon calculators to determine your share of the CO_2 emitted by the aircraft. (The best of these calculators will consider such factors as the total distance, the increased warming impact of emissions at high altitude, the aircraft type, how full it was, and whether the flight was direct or involved a stopover, but most are much less sophisticated.) In this example, you might find that you were responsible for 3.5 tons of CO_2 emissions. You would then pay a carbon offset company for 3.5 tons of CO_2 offsets. The company (or nonprofit organization) would then invest your money in a project meant to reduce greenhouse gas emissions and you get credit for a share equal to the carbon you were responsible for on your flight.

SOURCE: Anja Kollmuss, "Carbon Offsets 101," Worldwatch Institute, June 14, 2007.

tion: It would give businesses a reason to invest in new equipment and facilities even in the face of excess capacity. And given the current state of the economy [a recession], that's just what the doctor ordered. This short-run economic boost isn't the main reason to move on climate-change policy. The important thing is that the planet is in danger, and the longer we wait the worse it gets."[11]

People who oppose CO_2 cap-and-trade legislation, which includes many conservatives and business groups, believe it will increase the costs of energy, kill jobs, and damage the American economy. An editorial from the *Wall Street Journal* on June 26, 2009, expresses the sentiment of many who oppose CO_2 cap and trade:

> The whole point of cap and trade is to hike the price of electricity and gas so that Americans will use less. These higher prices will show up not just in electricity bills or at the gas station but in every manufactured good, from food to cars. Consumers will cut back on spending, which in turn will cut back on production, which results in fewer jobs created or higher unemployment. Some companies will instead move their operations overseas, with the same result. Americans should know that this is likely to be the biggest tax in American history.[12]

Carbon Taxes

Some people think that the most efficient and simplest approach to reducing CO_2 emissions is to place a tax on them and give power generators, industrial manufacturers, and individual automobile owners a financial incentive to cut back on their energy consumption or buy cleaner technologies. Under a carbon tax, Congress would levy a fee for each ton of CO_2 emitted or for each ton of carbon contained in fossil fuels, that is, coal, oil, and natural gas. Carbon taxes could be levied at any point along the route of commerce starting upstream from the point where fossil fuels are imported or domestically produced all the way downstream to the point where they are consumed and where CO_2 enters the atmosphere. The revenues generated from the tax could be used by the government in many ways, such as to support the development of renewable or alternative energy or help consumers deal with higher energy prices. Many advocates of carbon taxes suggest that revenues from the tax could be used to reform the income tax system by reducing the tax burden on labor, investment, and capital. According to the Carbon Tax Center (CTC), an organization dedicated to promoting the virtues of the tax approach, carbon taxes are superior to cap and trade for several reasons. The CTC says that carbon taxes are more predictable, easier to implement and understand, and less prone to manipulation by special interests. Furthermore, the organization says that carbon tax revenues are more likely be returned to the public through dividends or progressive tax-shifting, whereas the costs of cap-and-trade systems are likely to become a hidden tax as dollars flow to market participants, lawyers, and consultants.[13]

Many other people think that carbon taxes are not viable in the United States. In an article in the journal for the University of Pennsylvania's Wharton School of Business, Eric Orts, director of Wharton's Initiative for Global Environmental Leadership, states, "If you just look at the general issue from a pure academic and economic point of view, then many people are supportive of taxes—without considering the politics. As a theoretical matter, there's a lot to be said for taxes. But practically, I think, there are a lot of reasons it is not viable right now. First, 'tax' is a four-letter word in the United States."[14]

The cap-and-trade approach has been more popular in the U.S. Congress than a carbon tax. Seven cap-and-trade bills and only two carbon-tax bills were introduced in the 110th Congress (2007–2008). In the 111th Congress (2009–2010), the American Clean Energy and Security Act, which would establish a CO_2 cap-and-trade program, took center stage. In his 2010 State of the Union address, in the midst of record high unemployment, President Barack Obama said the country needs to create more clean energy jobs because the nation that leads the clean energy economy will be the nation that leads the global economy. Citing the American Clean Energy and Security Act as being part of this effort, he urged Congress to take the final steps toward establishing a national CO_2 cap-and-trade program.

Notes

1. Piers Forster, Venkatachalam Ramaswamy et al., "Changes in Atmospheric Constituents and in Radiative Forcing," in *Climate Change 2007:The Physical Science Basis, Contribution of Working Group I to the Fourth Assessment Report of the Intergovernmental Panel on Climate Change*, ed. Susan Solomon et al., New York: Cambridge University Press, 2007.
2. *Clean Air Act*, U.S. *Code* 42, § 7602.
3. *Massachusetts et al. v. Environmental Protection Agency et al.*, Supreme Court of the United States, April 2, 2007, p. 30.
4. *Massachusetts et al. v. Environmental Protection Agency et al*, p. 65.
5. U.S. Environmental Protection Agency, "Proposed Endangerment and Cause or Contribute Findings for Greenhouse Gases Under the Clean Air Act," April 17, 2009. www.epa.gov.
6. U.S. Small Business Administration, "Comments on EPA's 'Proposed Endangerment and Cause or Contribute Findings for Greenhouse Gases Under Section 202(a) of the Clean Air Act," June 23, 2009. www.sba.gov.
7. Quoted in Bryan Walsh, "The EPA's Move to Regulate Carbon: A Stopgap Solution," *Time*, February 20, 2009.
8. Kevin Knobloch, "Carbon Dioxide: Should EPA Wait on Congress?" *National Journal*, February 2, 2009. http://energy.nationaljournal.com.
9. William Nordhaus, "Economic Issues in Designing Global Agreement on Global Warming," keynote address for *Climate Change: Global Risks, Challenges, and Decisions*, Copenhagen, Denmark, March 10-12, 2009. http://nordhaus.econ.yale.edu.
10. Environmental Defense Fund, "The Cap and Trade Success Story," updated May 26, 2009. www.edf.org.
11. Paul Krugman, "An Affordable Salvation," *New York Times*, May 1, 2009.
12. *Wall Street Journal*, "The Cap and Tax Fiction," June 26, 2009.
13. Carbon Tax Center, "Tax vs. Cap-Trade," updated April 2009. www.carbontax.org.
14. Quoted in Knowledge@Wharton, "Carbon Cutting with Cap and Trade: A 'Step in the Right Direction, but . . . Far from Ideal," May 27, 2009. http://knowledge.wharton.upenn.edu.

CHAPTER 5

Reducing Automobile Emissions

A s a group, cars and trucks are the second biggest source of carbon dioxide emissions in the United States. Each year the U.S. government Research and Innovation Technology Administration (RITA) collects statistics on the number of vehicles in the nation, the number of miles these vehicles are driven, how much fuel they consume, and many other transportation-related statistics. A look at some of these statistics reveals that driving accounts for a large amount of CO_2 emissions. According to RITA, close to 237.4 million cars, vans, SUVs, and pickup trucks were registered in the United States in 2007; Americans traveled nearly 3 trillion miles (4.82 trillion kilometers) in these vehicles and consumed more than 136 billion gallons (515 billion liters) of fuel.[1] According to the U.S. Environmental Protection Agency (EPA), about 19 pounds (8.6 kg) of CO_2 are emitted for every gallon of gas consumed by American drivers.[2] The RITA statistics reveal that the average passenger car driver contributes to climate change by emitting more than 10,000 pounds (4,536 kg) of CO_2 each year.

The government can do several things to reduce the transportation sector's CO_2 emissions and help stave off global warming. First, the government can reduce the amount of miles Americans drive to work, school, or shopping. Second the government can increase the efficiency of individual vehicles by requiring that vehicles squeeze more miles out of a gallon of gasoline. Third, the government can try to get automakers and other manufacturers to invest in, and Americans to use, alternative vehicles and alternative fuels that emit less CO_2 into the atmosphere.

The average passenger car driver contributes to climate change by emitting more than 10,000 pounds of CO_2 each year.

Getting Americans to Drive Less

The federal government can help local government leaders develop their cities and counties in ways that encourage people to drive less. Local communities control development through planning strategies and zoning ordinances. The EPA "Smart Growth" initiative provides tools for local governments to use to develop their communities more compactly so that people do not have to drive long distances to get to work, school, or shopping. Smart Growth development supports safe and pleasant walking, biking, and accessible public transit, which allow people to get around more easily without a car. A study published in 2008 by the Urban Land Institute examined the vehicle miles traveled and CO_2 emissions in different communities to determine how more compact and efficient development patterns could help reduce the transportation sector's impact on the climate. The study concluded that compact development could reduce vehicle miles traveled by 20 to 40 percent and reduce CO_2 emissions by 7 to 10 percent by 2050, compared to conventional development patterns.[3] In addition to the Smart Growth initiative, in June 2009, the EPA joined with the U.S. Department of Housing and Urban Development and the U.S. Department of Transportation to create a Partnership for Sustainable Communities, which is to coordinate federal housing, transportation, and other infrastructure investments to protect

U.S. TRANSPORTATION EMISSIONS PER CAPITA BY STATE

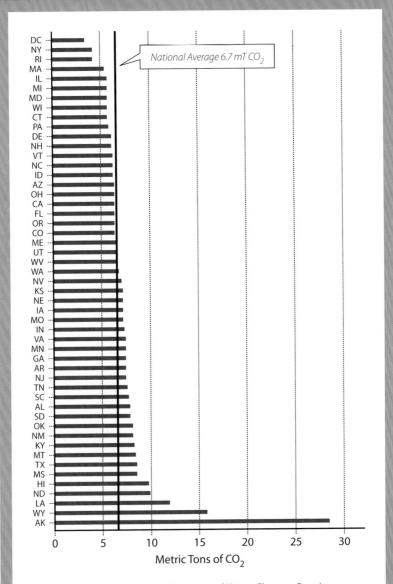

National Average 6.7 mT CO$_2$

Metric Tons of CO$_2$

Source: Elizabeth Stanton, Frank Ackerman, and Kristen Sheeran, *Greenhouse Gases and the American Lifestyle: Understanding Interstate Differences in Emissions*, Portland, OR: Ecotrust, 2009.

the environment, promote equitable development, and help address the challenges of climate change.

Convincing Americans to drive less can reduce CO_2 emissions by a small percentage in the long term. Driving is a part of the American culture, however. Acknowledging this fact, the government has sought to reduce the impact of individual cars on the road by making them more efficient.

Making Cars More Efficient

The government first started regulating the efficiency of vehicle engines in response to the 1973 oil crisis. In October 1973, the flow of Mideast oil into the United States slowed to a trickle as OPEC (the Organization of Petroleum Exporting Countries) stopped sending oil to the country in retaliation for U.S. support of Israel in the Yom Kippur War. Americans who remember the 1973 OPEC oil embargo recall long lines at the gas pump and high gasoline prices. The crisis was a decisive moment in the country's energy policy. Many new laws were enacted after the crisis, and "renewable energy" entered the vocabulary of the American public.

One of the laws that Congress enacted after the oil crisis was the Energy Policy and Conservation Act of 1975. Its goal was to save energy and reduce the country's dependence on foreign oil. Among other things, the act established the Corporate Average Fuel Economy (CAFE) program, which requires that cars and light-duty trucks sold in the United States meet certain mile per gallon (mpg) standards for how far they can run on a gallon of gasoline. The Congress set the standard for cars initially at 18 mpg beginning with automobile model year (MY) 1978. This figure ratcheted up steadily to 27.5 mpg by MY 1985, where it has remained since then. For light-duty trucks, a class that includes sport utility vehicles (SUVs), minivans, and pickups, the standard started out ranging from 15.8 to 17.2 mpg in 1979 and increased to 22.2 mpg by 2007.

The Debate over CAFE Standards

In December 2007, the Energy Independence and Security Act of 2007 was enacted into law with a provision to increase CAFE standards for MYs 2011–2020. The law instructs the U.S. Department of Transportation to increase fuel economy standards each year so that, by 2020, the combined average fuel economy of all passenger cars, pickup trucks, vans, and SUVs will be at least 35 mpg.

Before the law was enacted, the CAFE provisions were contentiously debated. Automakers and others opposed to the provisions argued that the CAFE standards are not effective in reducing CO_2 emissions or lessening U.S. dependence on foreign oil. They say that when consumers drive more efficient cars, they tend to drive more, which offsets any benefits gained from increased fuel economy. According to Jerry Taylor and Peter Van Doren, senior fellows at the Cato Institute, "increasing CAFE standards will not decrease the amount of pollution coming from the U.S. auto fleet. That's because we regulate emissions per mile traveled, not per gallon of gasoline burned. Improvements in fuel efficiency reduce the cost of driving and thus increase vehicle miles traveled."[4] Other arguments voiced against increasing CAFE standards focused on the impact to domestic automakers and restrictions on consumer choice. Eric Peters, senior fellow at the National Center of Public Policy, contends that CAFE standards disproportionately hurt American car companies because these manufacturers make most of their profits by selling large pickup trucks and SUVs, which would probably require substantial retooling to meet the increased standards. Peters says this gives a competitive leg-up to foreign automakers, which make most of their money selling smaller, easier-to-retool and inherently more economical passenger cars. According to Peters, "GM, Ford and Chrysler have all posted alarming losses recently, even as the quality and appeal of their vehicles has been on the upswing. Hitting them with a 35-mpg fuel economy edict would have the same effect as sucker punching someone already laid low by the flu."[5] Peters also argues that consumers should have a choice of buying low-mpg vehicles because sometimes size, power, and capability—which are sacrificed in high-mpg vehicles—are needed. Says Peters, "you can't tow 9,000 pounds with a Camry. Sometimes, miles-per-gallon is not the sole reason for buying a vehicle."[6]

Groups that favored increased CAFE standards included the Pew Charitable Trusts and the Union of Concerned Scientists (UCS). According to the Pew Campaign for Fuel Efficiency, the newly enacted CAFE provisions, "will save 1.1 million barrels of oil a day and $25 billion for consumers at the pump—making the auto industry the first major sector of the American economy that will reduce its global warming pollution by the equivalent of taking 28 million cars off the road."[7] Many environmental groups contend the increased CAFE standards will reduce the transportation sector's contribution to climate change by lowering CO_2 emissions, and some of these groups also believe that CAFE standards can benefit the economy. UCS maintains that automakers already have the technology to build more efficient vehicles and that they can do so cost-effectively. Furthermore, the group believes that CAFE standards can create more auto manufacturing jobs. According to the UCS,

> A fleet of cars and light trucks that reaches 35 mpg will cost about $1,000 to $2,000 extra per vehicle. This additional cost will be more than offset by the fuel savings consumers will enjoy over the life of the vehicle. Consumer fuel savings along with automaker investment to produce a 35-mpg fleet by 2020 will help spur the creation of more than 170,800 new jobs in the year 2020.[8]

For their part, Detroit automakers seem committed to meeting the new CAFE standards. After its bankruptcy proceedings in 2009, Chrysler indicated it will rely on its relationship with Italian automaker Fiat to develop a nationwide fleet of low-emission, fuel-efficient vehicles. Several months after GM survived its own bankruptcy, the company issued the following statement on the new CAFE standards:

> A strong, single national fuel economy standard will benefit consumers and automakers alike by helping get more clean and efficient vehicles on the road quickly and more affordably. Greater consistency and certainty among a variety of regulations will help a new GM execute its current product plan centered on new technologies and more highly fuel-efficient and quality cars and trucks.[9]

Similarly, Ford Motor Co. said the new CAFE standards "will provide one clear requirement for increasing fuel economy and provide greater certainty for our product planning."[10]

Many environmentalists argue that combatting global warming requires the government to do more than just increase vehicle fuel economy standards. They suggest the internal combustion engine should be phased out and the government should support the development and commercialization of alternative vehicles and alternative fuels.

Promoting Alternative Vehicles and Fuels

A wide range of alternative vehicles is being developed to replace ones using the conventional internal combustion engine (ICE). They include vehicles that are powered by modified ICEs and vehicles that lack an engine altogether. Flex fuel vehicles have slightly modified ICEs and can accept gasoline and 85 percent ethanol fuels. Natural gas vehicles have modified ICEs that run on liquefied natural gas. Hybrid electric vehicles combine an internal combustion engine with battery powered operation. Electric vehicles and fuel cell vehicles do away with the ICE completely and are powered by batteries or fuel cells.

Getting these vehicles on the road is an intensive process. Manufacturers have to develop prototypes that they can actually build and people can eventually buy for reasonable prices. Sup-

Slowing Climate Change by Plugging Into the Grid

There is a growing consensus that America's dependence on oil constitutes a triple threat to its national security, its economic vitality, and its environmental health. But agreement breaks down on the question of how, exactly, the country can best achieve dramatic, near-term reductions in oil consumption. We believe that the greatest potential for transformative change may lie in the emerging technology of plug-in hybrid-electric vehicles (PHEVs), which could become widely available in the United States in five to 10 years if government takes a few smart steps to help spur their commercialization.

Like conventional hybrid-electric vehicles, plug-in hybrids save fuel by using small internal combustion engines in combination with electric motors. But while conventional hybrids charge their batteries with kinetic energy and power generated by their own internal combustion engines, plug-in hybrids, as the name suggests, have cords that can be plugged into standard, 120-volt electrical outlets.

That design—constituting a partial merger of the transportation and electricity sectors—can produce dramatic reductions in gasoline

porting infrastructures to provide fuel and maintenance must also be developed. Additionally, consumer attitudes may also need changing to accept new vehicles.

One of the first ways the government can promote alternative vehicles is to help manufacturers develop them. The U.S. government has provided research funding and incentives to auto manufacturers to develop many different alternative vehicles. For example, the government spurred the manufacture of more flex fuel vehicles with the Alternative Motor Fuels Act of 1988, which gave automakers credits toward meeting CAFE standards based on how many flex fuel vehicles they produced. Carmakers could make more gas-guzzling trucks and SUVs if they manu-

consumption. Equipped with more powerful battery packs than conventional hybrids, plug-in hybrids can travel the first 20 miles or more on battery power alone, without ever firing up their internal combustion engines. That is farther than the average round-trip commute. After that, they can switch to a conventional hybrid-electric operating mode. In all-around driving, plug-ins could thus get between 80 m.p.g. and 160 m.p.g., compared to about 45 m.p.g. for today's Toyota Prius. The gasoline savings could be even greater if plug-ins were designed to run on biofuels; they could travel 500 miles on a gallon of gasoline blended with five gallons of ethanol.

Even beyond the possible reductions in oil consumption, plug-ins also offer a compounded benefit in their ability to sharply reduce carbon dioxide emissions and thus slow global warming. The beauty is in the increased reliance on the electricity grid, which can concentrate the environmental impact of driving upstream in a few thousand electrical power plants instead of downstream in a hundred million motor vehicles. That puts the environmental policy focus squarely on reducing greenhouse gas emissions from the power sector, where there is the greatest opportunity to make high-volume progress.

SOURCE: Joseph Romm and Peter Fox-Penner, "Plugging Into the Grid," Progressive Policy Institute, March 2007.

factured flex fuel vehicles. Before the law's passage there were very few flex fuel vehicles on the road. By 2006, it was estimated that there were from 4 million to 5 million registered flex fuel vehicles in the country.[11]

The law had a significant loophole though, which appeared to undermine its strategy. Although the flex fuel vehicles *could* be fueled with up to 85 percent ethanol, most people who bought the cars found it very difficult to find fueling stations offering ethanol. So they ended up using strictly gasoline and their cars consumed the same amount of gasoline—and emitted the same amount of CO_2—as conventional cars. According to Phil Lampert, executive director of the National Ethanol Vehicle Co-

Initiatives such as 2009's American Recovery and Reinvestment Act encouraged automakers to research and manufacture nonpolluting electric cars such as the Chevrolet Volt, shown here with Michigan governor Jennifer Granholm. AP Images.

alition, "while the Alternative Motor Fuels Act provided an incentive for automakers to build the cars, it did not address the development of an infrastructure for the fuel."[12]

The U.S. federal government tried to make ethanol fuel more accessible and available when the Congress created the Renewable Fuel Standard program in 2005. The program initially required that 4 billion gallons of renewable fuels, primarily ethanol, be added to the U.S. fuel supply in 2006. In 2007, lawmakers increased the volume of renewable fuel required to be blended into gasoline from 9 billion gallons (34 billion liters) in 2008 to 36 billion gallons (136 billion liters) by 2022. This shift would offset only a fraction of U.S. gasoline consumption. The U.S. Energy Information Administration estimates that Americans consume 380 million gallons (1.4 billion liters) of gasoline every day, almost 140 billion gallons (530 billion liters) annually.[13]

Many people question the wisdom of promoting ethanol and flex fuel vehicles as a climate change mitigation strategy. Some scientists contend that it takes more energy—in the form of coal, oil, natural gas, and electricity—to make a gallon of ethanol than actually comes from burning it. Additionally, studies show that the primary process of making ethanol today, which uses corn as a feedstock (raw material), reduces greenhouse gas emissions only moderately when compared to gasoline. Some of these issues might be resolved if cellulosic materials, such as paper and wood debris, were used as the feedstock instead of corn. The U.S. Department of Energy has devised a strategy to displace 30 percent of the nation's current gasoline use with ethanol derived from cellulose-based feedstocks by 2030.

Flex fuel vehicles are the most commercialized of the different types of alternative fuel vehicles, but the federal government and automobile manufacturers are devoting significant resources to get other alternative vehicles on the road. The American Recovery and Reinvestment Act of 2009 contained billions of dollars in grants for battery manufacturers to develop advanced batteries for electric and hybrid electric vehicles, such as GM's Chevy Volt plug-in hybrid electric vehicle.

Groups and organizations focused on climate change mitigation think that the transportation sector's contribution to climate change can be significantly reduced by combining the strategies described above along with national CO_2 regulations of some type. In a report for the Pew Center on Global Climate Change, David Greene from Oak Ridge National Laboratory and Andreas Schafer from the Massachusetts Institute of Technology state that, in order to reduce greenhouse gas emissions related to transportation,

> we need a mix of policies. Opportunities for significant emission reductions include implementing a carbon constraint, raising efficiency standards for automobiles, blending low-carbon fuels with gasoline, and changing land-use patterns through urban design and planning. Each of these measures could contribute to reducing greenhouse gas emissions, but none is sufficient alone.[14]

Notes

1. U.S. Department of Transportation, Research and Innovative Technology Administration, Bureau of Transportation Statistics, *National Transportation Statistics*, 2009. www.bts.gov.
2. U.S. Environmental Protection Agency, "Emission Facts: Average Carbon Dioxide Emissions Resulting from Gasoline and Diesel Fuel," EPA420-F-05-001, February 2005. www.epa.gov.
3. Reid Ewing et al., *Growing Cooler*, Washington, DC: Urban Land Institute, 2008.
4. Jerry Taylor and Peter Van Doren, "Don't Raise CAFE Standards," *National Review Online*, August 1, 2007.
5. Eric Peters, "No to New Fuel Economy Standards: Consumer Choice, Not Congress, Should Drive Detroit's Decisionmaking," *National Policy Analysis*, June 2007. www.nationalcenter.org.
6. Peters, "No to New Fuel Economy Standards."
7. Pew Charitable Trusts Environment Group, "Pew Campaign for Fuel Efficiency," 2008. www.pewfuelefficiency.org.
8. Union of Concerned Scientists, "Fuel Economy Basics," www.ucsusa.org.
9. General Motors, "General Motors Statement Regarding Joint EPA/NHTSA NPRM On Fuel Economy/GHG Emissions," September 15, 2009. www.gm.com.
10. Ford Motor Co., "Ford Comment on Congressional Passage of New CAFE Standards and the Energy Bill," December 18, 2007. http://media.ford.com.
11. American Petroleum Institute, "Backgrounder on Flexible Fuel Vehicles and E85," March 23, 2006. www.api.org.
12. Quoted in Tara Baukus Mello, "Fueling Up with Ethanol," Edmunds.com, July 5, 2007. www.edmunds.com.
13. U.S. Energy Information Administration, "Gasoline Explained," May 5, 2010. http://tonto.eia.doe.gov.
14. David Greene and Andreas Schafer, "Reducing Greenhouse Gas Emissions from U.S. Transportation," Pew Center on Global Climate Change, May 2003.

CHAPTER 6

Making Buildings More Energy Efficient

G overnments can help prevent global warming by implementing policies that reduce the amount of energy consumed by
buildings. It is estimated that about 40 percent of all the energy
consumed and 40 percent of all the carbon dioxide (CO_2) emitted into the air in the United States are associated with heating, cooling, running appliances and electronics, and providing
lighting for buildings.[1] Therefore, making buildings more energy
efficient is an important part of government climate change reduction efforts.

State governments, with guidance and direction from the
federal government, are generally responsible for trying to reduce the energy consumed by buildings in the United States.
States have used four main strategies to cut the amount of energy
buildings consume. First, state building codes require that newly
constructed buildings are designed to reduce wasted energy and
are built with energy-efficient materials. Second, most states have
energy-efficiency programs requiring electric and gas utilities to
lower the energy consumption of existing buildings. Third, the
U.S. government gives money to states to help weatherize the
homes of low-income people, thus reducing their utility bills and
saving energy. Finally, the U.S. government and the states have
adopted standards that require appliances and electronic devices
be manufactured to consume no more than a specified level of
energy. States have used these and other policies to reduce the

amount of energy consumed by buildings, cut CO_2 emissions, and help avoid climate change.

State Energy Codes: Ensuring New Buildings Are Energy Efficient

As with many other energy-saving policies, state energy codes for buildings began in the 1970s, largely as a result of energy crises that occurred during that time. In 1978, an amendment to the federal Energy Policy and Conservation Act was passed requiring states receiving financial assistance from the federal government to establish an energy code, or a set of laws specifying certain energy efficiency measures, which must be installed in new residential and commercial buildings. Generally energy codes require that buildings are sealed and insulated to specific levels of thermal resistance, heating and cooling equipment meets certain efficiency levels, energy-efficient lighting is installed, windows meet certain thermal specifications, and options are provided for renewable energy such as solar panels or geothermal heating systems. The 1978 amendment did not specify what standards states should adopt in their energy codes, only that a state have an energy code.

It is estimated that about 40 percent of all the energy consumed and 40 percent of all the carbon dioxide (CO_2) emitted into the air in the United States are associated with . . . buildings.

In 1992, the U.S. Congress decided that state energy codes should at least meet minimum levels of energy efficiency. The Congress called on the U.S. Department of Energy to judge the effectiveness of model energy codes, which are established by building and energy experts at nongovernmental organizations such as the American Society of Heating, Refrigerating, and Air-conditioning Engineers (ASHRAE) and the International Code Council (ICC). Every three years or so, ASHRAE publishes a model energy code applicable to commercial buildings, whereas ICC issues a model energy code for residential buildings. Under the federal Energy Policy Act of 1992, states are required to adopt the ASHRAE commercial code and to *consider* the ICC model energy code, if they are deemed effective by the Department of Energy—which they consistently have been.

Despite the federal laws, not all states have residential energy codes or have residential codes that meet the federal minimum levels of efficiency. According to the Alliance to Save Energy, ten states, including Alabama, Arizona, Colorado, Maine, and Wyoming, still do not have residential energy codes. Other states, such as Indiana, Michigan, Minnesota, and Tennessee have codes that are not as effective as the ICC's. According to Lowell Unger of the Alliance to Save Energy, if these states improved their codes to be like the codes in California, Georgia, Ohio, Pennsylvania, or Wisconsin, by 2030 the country could save 8 percent of total building energy use, $28 billion in consumer energy bills, and avoid 250 million tons of CO_2 emissions.[2]

Many people think that climate change concerns make it imperative that the U.S. government create its own national model energy code and require states to meet it. According to Lane Burt of the Natural Resources Defense Council, "In the context of global climate change, reducing emissions today and emissions in 2050 are critically important. The buildings we build today can last for a century or more and we can't continue to put off efficiency and waste energy. Just think of the 25 years of inefficient homes we could have avoided if a national code had been implemented in the 1980s, when the discussions first began. Let's stop making the same mistakes and thinking the problem will take care of itself."[3] Burt and others are hoping that the 111th U.S. Congress passes, and the president signs, legislation to create a national model energy code and set energy savings goals for buildings.

Not everyone thinks a national energy code is needed to fight climate change. Home builders in particular say that homes are

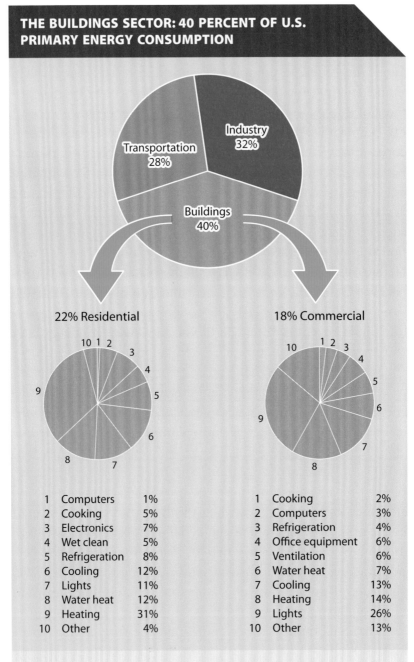

THE BUILDINGS SECTOR: 40 PERCENT OF U.S. PRIMARY ENERGY CONSUMPTION

Industry
32%

Transportation
28%

Buildings
40%

22% Residential

18% Commercial

	Residential	
1	Computers	1%
2	Cooking	5%
3	Electronics	7%
4	Wet clean	5%
5	Refrigeration	8%
6	Cooling	12%
7	Lights	11%
8	Water heat	12%
9	Heating	31%
10	Other	4%

	Commercial	
1	Cooking	2%
2	Computers	3%
3	Refrigeration	4%
4	Office equipment	6%
5	Ventilation	6%
6	Water heat	7%
7	Cooling	13%
8	Heating	14%
9	Lights	26%
10	Other	13%

Source: David E. Rodgers, "Building Energy Codes as a Response to Climate Change," The Senate Committee on Energy and Natural Resources, April 30, 2008.

already built efficiently and establishing a national energy code would only hurt an already struggling sector of the U.S. economy. This law would make it harder for average Americans to purchase homes, they say. Sonny Richardson, a home builder from Tuscaloosa, Alabama, testified against the need for a national energy code in front of a House or Representatives committee in April 2009. Richardson said that the home-building industry has suffered "devastating losses and historic declines" that would only be exacerbated by a national energy code, and that mandating energy codes "may not achieve true energy savings, but are likely to impair affordability for millions of future residents of green and energy-efficient dwellings." Richardson also said that "the ability to realize additional energy savings from an already super-efficient segment of the residential sector via building codes is extremely limited, and thus cannot be expected to deliver dramatic results in terms of greenhouse gas emissions reductions or consumer utility savings." Richardson, who was speaking on behalf of the National Association of Home Builders, suggested that the best way to achieve the goals of reducing energy consumption and greenhouse gas emissions is to focus on existing homes rather than new homes.[4]

Reducing Energy Consumption in Existing Buildings

States primarily use energy efficiency programs to lower the energy consumption of existing buildings. Typically, state energy efficiency programs require electric and gas utilities to reduce the amount of energy they sell. For instance, in 2004, California required its large utilities to reduce the amount of electricity and gas they sell by 1 percent each year until 2013.[5] In order to meet the energy savings requirements, utilities generally go out to customers' homes or businesses and perform energy audits to pinpoint areas where energy is being wasted, check the efficiency of heating and cooling systems, and look for ways to save electricity. Utilities also offer rebates to customers for purchasing

California Is a Leader on Climate Policies

In politics and policy at large, the time is long past when the nation routinely looked to California, as it did in the 1960s and the '70s, as the most fertile incubator of new ideas. On many fronts, the state government appears almost dysfunctional, hobbled by constitutional constraints and partisan polarization. The collapse of the state's (latest) real-estate bubble has sent California's economy into free fall. A short list of the state's current problems would include surging unemployment, struggling schools, and a budget deficit larger than the entire budget in almost every other state.

But on energy and climate change, the story is very different. Ever since the first Arab oil embargo, in 1973, California has consistently defined the forward edge of energy-policy innovation in America. In 2006, California's per capita energy consumption was the fourth-lowest in the country. The state emits only about half as much carbon per dollar of economic activity as the rest of America. It generates significantly more electricity than any other state from non-hydroelectric renewable energy sources like solar, wind, and biomass. California registers more patents associated with clean energy than any other state and attracts most of the venture capital invested in U.S. "cleantech" companies exploring everything from electric cars to solar power generation.

energy-efficient appliances, and they educate consumers about the value of saving energy. The money required to establish energy efficiency programs and provide the rebates is typically collected by a surcharge of a few dollars a month on each customer's energy bill.

According to the American Council for an Energy Efficient Economy, California has one of the best state energy efficiency programs in the country. In 2009, the California Public Utilities Commission (CPUC) announced that it is requiring utilities to reduce energy consumption by more than 1.5 percent per year from 2010 to 2012, or 5 percent overall. The CPUC says

"I unequivocally believe we are a model for the rest of the country," says F. Noel Perry, the founder of Next10, a nonpartisan Silicon Valley–based think tank, whose "California Green Innovation Index" studies have tracked these trends.

Some of California's edge can be traced to the state's natural advantages, particularly a temperate climate that does not require as much heating in the winter or cooling in the summer as do many other parts of the country. But the difference is also rooted in conscious policy decisions. The American Council for an Energy-Efficient Economy, a leading nonprofit research group, recently ranked California first among the states in promoting energy efficiency.

"California has fouled up plenty of things," said John Bryson, the former chairman of both the California Public Utilities Commission and Southern California Edison, the major Los Angeles–area utility that is a national leader in energy efficiency. "But on this set of issues—the clean-energy issues, the kind of things that need to be done in terms of the risk of climate change—I think California is getting it right. . . . More than any other state I know of, California has done already most of the things that need to be done."

SOURCE: Ronald Brownstein, "The California Experiment," *Atlantic*, October 2009. www.energy.ca.gov.

the goal will create energy savings equivalent to the output of three medium-size power plants and will avoid 3 million tons of greenhouse gas emissions.[6] In order to achieve the energy reduction goals, CPUC is allowing utilities to collect $3.1 billion from California ratepayers in the form of extra fees tacked onto their electricity bills over the three-year period.

Despite their belief that everything must be done to fight global warming, many people in California are worried by the large tab for energy efficiency programs and the fact that utilities are in charge. Rebecca Bowe, writing in the *San Francisco Bay Guardian* in April 2009, sums up this concern:

As the window of opportunity for averting the worst-case global warming scenarios narrows, wise use of energy seems increasingly urgent. So millions of dollars in state and federal funding and significant contributions from utility customers are devoted each year to improving energy efficiency in California. It's a crucial program designed to reduce consumption and planet-damaging emissions and eliminate the need for new fossil-fuel burning power plants. Yet the state's energy-efficiency programs are often run by investor-owned utility companies, such as Pacific Gas & Electric, that have been missing efficiency targets yet demanding ever more public money anyway.[7]

Energy efficiency programs generally receive a lot of money from the federal government. The Energy Efficiency and Conservation Block Grant is a federal program, created by the U.S. Congress in 2007, that provides grants to states, Indian tribes, cities, and counties to implement programs that reduce energy use and fossil-fuel emissions and improve energy efficiency. Some states and cities are using the federal money to provide low-interest loans to help consumers install energy-efficient appliances in their homes. For instance, the state of Michigan and the city of Portland, Oregon, give homeowners access to low-interest, long-term financing to buy energy-efficient furnaces, air conditioners, and other appliances. Homeowners will be able to pay back the cost of the appliances over time through a small charge on their utility bills. Portland Mayor Sam Adams touted the environmental and economic benefits of his city's Clean Energy Fund in his state-of-the-city address in February 2009. Said Adams, "once the loan is paid off, the homeowner keeps the monthly savings, all the while enjoying the benefits of a more comfortable,

---

Following page: Since 1978, the U.S. federal government has required states to have energy codes covering construction standards—such as the inclusion of these solar panels on the roof of a Sam's Club store in California. David McNew/Getty Images.

more efficient, and more valuable home. This creates jobs now and keeps money in Portland in the long run. It is a critical part of the City's Climate Protection Strategy and a great example of how we can reduce carbon emissions while strengthening our local economy."[8]

Weatherization Programs Help Reduce Energy Use

For many years the federal government has given money to states to help weatherize the homes of low-income Americans, particularly senior citizens. Weatherization is a type of energy efficiency that deals primarily with keeping cold air out of homes by insulating, installing storm windows and doors, caulking cracks and applying weatherstripping. In 1976 Congress created the Weatherization Assistance Program (WAP) to help low-income Americans struggling with high heating bills due to the 1973 energy crisis. The government created the program because high energy bills are particularly difficult for people on fixed incomes to handle. According to the U.S. Department of Energy, "Although the 1973 oil crisis affected the pocketbooks of most Americans for years, its impact on low-income households was much more dramatic than on other groups. For some families, suddenly ballooning home heating bills threw them into debt and even into poverty."[9] The Department of Energy started giving states money to help vulnerable families save money on heating bills by sending contractors to their homes to seal doors, windows, and other leaks where costly heated air poured out and cold air entered. The department says that the WAP weatherizes about one hundred thousand low-income households each year and saves each homeowner $350 on average in reduced heating bills.[10] Additionally, the average home that the WAP serves burns 32 percent less natural gas for heating and emits 1.62 fewer metric tons of CO_2 yearly, according to the nonprofit organization Economic Opportunity Studies of Washington, D.C.[11] The WAP helps low-income households reduce their heating costs and helps reduce greenhouse gas emissions.

Appliance Standards: Building Energy-Efficient Appliances

Whereas weatherization focuses on maintaining the interior temperature of homes, appliance standards focus on ensuring refrigerators, washing machines, dishwashers, and other appliances are built to use as little energy as practical. California enacted the first appliance standards in the country in the 1970s, and soon several other states followed suit with their own standards. Appliance manufacturers had to make sure their products met a patchwork of different state standards. Manufacturers were generally relieved when the federal government enacted the National Appliance Energy Conservation Act (NAECA) of 1987 and set national standards. NAECA established standards for refrigerators, freezers, air conditioners, dishwashers, and most other common household products. A few years after NAECA was enacted, the U.S. Environmental Protection Agency began the Energy Star program to identify products that are the most energy efficient.

In 2009, California created a stir when state regulators announced that big-screen TVs would have to meet new state energy standards. The new standards require that big flat-screen HDTVs and plasma TVs, which an editorial in the *Silicon Valley Mercury News* called the "Hummers [a gas-guzzling brand of SUV] of consumer electronics" are built to conserve energy.[12] According to the California Energy Commission, "TVs consume 10 percent of a home's electricity. The TV energy standard will save consumers money on their electricity bill, conserve energy, protect the environment, help reduce greenhouse gas emissions and decrease the need to build additional, large power plants."[13] Some TV manufacturers have condemned the new standards. They say that they are building energy-efficient TVs on their own. These manufacturers contend that many TVs are already energy efficient enough to earn an Energy Star rating. They also think the standards could raise the cost of TVs and be economically harmful. In a 2009 *Los Angeles Times* article, Doug Johnson of the Consumer Electronics Association said, "Voluntary efforts are succeeding without regulations. Too much government interference could hamstring industry innovation and prove expensive to manufacturers and consumers."[14]

The TV manufacturers' argument that regulations to reduce energy and cut greenhouse gases are harmful to the economy is similar to the home builders' argument. This debate is a common one between regulators and industry in the determination of the government response to climate change and other environmental concerns. Typically, the government tries to strike a balance between responding to climate change concerns and respecting the economic viability of American businesses.

Notes

1. Lowell Ungar, "Building Energy Codes Prevent Climate Change," *Congressional Briefings*, April 30, 2008. http://ase.org.
2. Ungar, "Building Energy Codes Prevent Climate Change."
3. Lane Burt, "The Case for a National Building Energy Code," Natural Resources Defense Council, June 17, 2009.
4. Sonny Richardson, "Legislative Hearing Regarding American Clean Energy Security Act," Subcommittee on Energy and the Environment, House Energy and Commerce Committee, April 24, 2009. http://energycommerce.house.gov.
5. Maggie Eldridge et al., "The 2008 State Energy Efficiency Scorecard," American Council for an Energy Efficient Economy, October 2008, p. 23.
6. California Public Utilities Commission, "CPUC Makes Largest Commitment Ever Made by a State to Energy Efficiency," news release, September 24, 2009. www.cpuc.ca.gov.
7. Rebecca Bowe, "Green Issue: Utilities Miss Energy Efficiency Goals but Seek More Public Funds Anyway," *San Francisco Bay Guardian*, April 15, 2009. www.sfbg.com.
8. Quoted in Roy Kaufmann, "Mayor Adams Puts Forth Green Economic Development Strategy," Portlandonline, February 27, 2009. www.portlandonline.com.
9. U.S. Department of Energy, "Weatherization Assistance Program," July 8, 2010. www.energy.gov.
10. U.S. Department of Energy, Weatherization Assistance Program."
11. "The Weatherization Assistance Program Reduces Greenhouse Gas Emissions!" *Economic Opportunity Studies*. www.opportunitystudies.org.
12. "State Commission Should Approve Rules Cutting Flat-Screen TV Energy Use," *Silicon Valley Mercury News*, October 13, 2009. www.mercurynews.com.

13. California Energy Commission, "Frequently Asked Questions—Energy Efficiency Standards for Televisions," updated November 18, 2009. www.energy.ca.gov.
14. Quoted in Marc Lifsher, "California Appears Poised to Be First to Ban Power-Guzzling Big-Screen TVs," *Los Angeles Times*, October 14, 2009. www.latimes.com.

CHAPTER 7

Reducing Carbon Dioxide Emissions from Electricity Generation

Twenty-four hours a day and seven days a week, power plants provide the electricity modern humans arguably could not live without. In the United States, the majority of these power plants burn coal to make electricity. Coal is a rich fuel source and is abundant in the United States. Coal is known as a "dirty fuel," however, because harmful pollutants are released into the air when it is burned. As climate change concerns have increased, coal has gotten another bad mark: It is a major source of carbon dioxide (CO_2) emissions. Electricity generation is the single largest source of CO_2 in the United States. According to the U.S. Energy Information Administration, U.S. power plants emitted more than 2.5 billion tons of CO_2 into the air in 2007.[1] Reducing the amount of carbon dioxide coming from the production of electricity is a major aim of policy makers worried about climate change.

Responding to Climate Change with Renewable Energy

Carbon dioxide emissions from coal, as well as other fossil fuels, have caused policy makers to look more closely at renewable sources of power, such as wind, solar, and biomass energy. Wind energy uses spinning blades placed atop tall towers to convert the energy contained in the force of the wind into electric current. In solar energy systems, photovoltaic modules convert sun-

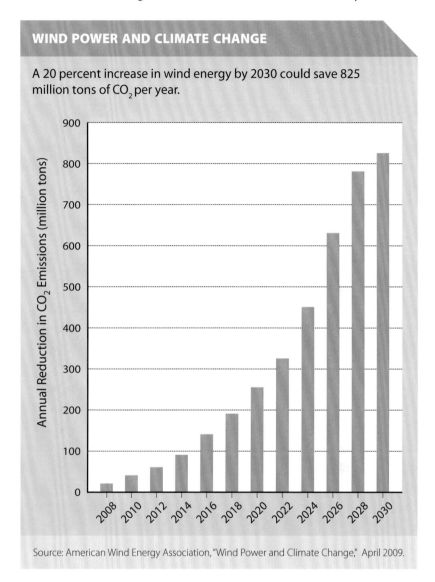

WIND POWER AND CLIMATE CHANGE

A 20 percent increase in wind energy by 2030 could save 825 million tons of CO_2 per year.

Source: American Wind Energy Association, "Wind Power and Climate Change," April 2009.

light into electric current similar to the way vegetation converts sunlight into chemical energy. Wind and solar are attractive to policy makers concerned about climate change because they have virtually zero emissions. Wind and solar energy systems are intermittent sources of energy, however, depending on the sun to shine or the wind to blow before they can generate electricity. Biomass energy is a form of renewable energy that is not intermittent, but it has greenhouse gas emissions, although generally lower than coal-generated power. Biomass energy systems take trash, animal manure, or other waste streams, and convert them into electricity or fuel by burning or microbial degradation, which uses bacteria to eat wastes and produce gases such as methane, which can be used as a fuel source. In general, anytime electricity is produced from renewable sources instead of coal, CO_2 emissions are lower.

Electricity generation is the single largest source of CO_2 in the United States.

Renewable energy technologies account for only a small fraction of U.S. electricity generation, but lawmakers are looking to increase this amount. According to the Energy Information Administration, less than 10 percent of all the electricity generated in the United States comes from renewable sources. Large-scale hydroelectric plants like those at Niagara Falls in New York and the Grand Coulee Dam in Washington account for about 7 percent of U.S. electricity. Solar, wind, and biomass energy combined accounted for a mere 2.3 percent of U.S. electricity generation in 2007.[2] According to a U.S. Department of Energy report, if the amount of wind energy alone was increased to 20 percent by 2030, a cumulative total of 7,600 million tons of CO_2 emissions would be avoided and more than 15,000 million tons of CO_2 emissions would be avoided through 2050.[3]

Spurring Investment in Renewable Energy

Bringing down the costs of renewable energy is a key part of government efforts to spur more investment in it. Part of the reason renewable technologies account for such a small amount of electricity generation is that they are generally more expensive. Since 1992, the federal government has provided tax credits for renewable energy in the hopes of lowering its costs and stimulating investment. The Production Tax Credit (PTC) program, established under the Energy Policy Act of 1992, provides tax credits to the owners or operators of wind, solar, or certain biomass energy systems based on how much energy these facilities produce. The more energy they make, the larger their tax credit. According to the American Wind Energy Association, the PTC has been "a critical factor in financing new wind farms."[4] In 2007, scientist Ryan Wiser and his colleagues at the Lawrence Berkeley National Laboratory analyzed the impact of the PTC on the wind energy business. They found that the PTC reduced the cost of wind power by roughly a third, making wind power more attractive to electric utilities and other investors. Testifying before the U.S. Senate Finance Committee in March 2007, Wiser stated that "it is difficult to overstate the importance of the PTC to the wind industry."[5]

Not everyone thinks the PTC is the best strategy to spur wind and other types of renewable development. Renewable industry analyst Paul Gipe has written extensively about renewable energy. He operates a Web site called Wind-works.org that promotes wind energy technology. Gipe thinks the PTC favors big businesses with large tax burdens at the expense of smaller wind developers. He also maintains the PTC is concentrating the wind energy business into the hands of only a few companies. Gipe suggests electricity feed laws, or feed-in tariffs, so called because they allow owners of renewable energy systems to "feed" energy to the electric grid, are much better ways to promote wind and other renewable energies. Feed-in tariff laws require utilities to

Following pages: The KFx coal thermal upgrading plant in Gillette, Wyoming, produces a cleaner burning coal known as K-Fuel. Robert Nickelsberg/Getty Images.

buy power from any renewable energy source offering it, at fixed prices determined by the government. This gives renewable energy developers confidence that they will be able to make a return on their investment and should spur investment. Feed-in tariffs have been adopted in more than forty countries and have been particularly successful in promoting wind energy development in Germany and Spain. According to Gipe, "it's time to jump off the Production Tax Credit treadmill and work toward a more open, transparent support mechanism [for renewable energy] such as the electricity feed law."[6] In the United States, California has implemented a feed-in tariff, and several other states are considering the policy.

Renewable energy portfolio standards have been a popular policy for promoting renewable energy in the United States. More than half the states have established renewable portfolio standards (RPS) as a market-friendly approach to spurring renewable energy projects. RPS policies promote renewable energy by requiring that electric utilities generate a certain portion of the electricity they sell from renewable energy sources. Under an RPS program, the government does not set the price of renewable energy and does not obligate utilities to buy power from any renewable energy source offering it, like feed-in tariffs do. However, RPS programs do require that a certain portion, generally from 7 to 30 percent, of the electricity sold by the utility be generated from renewable energy. The idea is that the government creates a demand for renewable energy but lets the market determine the prices.

So far the U.S. Congress has not established a nationwide RPS. Many states have, however. As of November 2009, twenty-nine states and the District of Columbia had enacted an RPS program, according to the Database of State Incentives for Renewables and Efficiency (DSIRE).[7] The Pew Center for Global Climate Change maintains RPS programs are a good way to combat the greenhouse effect. The Pew Center states that "although climate change may not be the prime motivation behind these

[RPS] standards, the use of renewable or alternative energy can deliver significant greenhouse gas reductions. Increasing a state's use of renewable energy brings other benefits as well, including job creation, energy security, and cleaner air."[8]

Some analysts suggest that the cost of electricity will increase if the amount of renewable energy is increased, whether by way of feed-in tariffs or RPS programs. According to a 2009 article in the *New York Times*, an analysis by a construction company specializing in energy projects found that wind is at least 50 percent more expensive than coal, if wind's intermittent nature is taken into account.[9] According to Glenn Schleede, an energy policy analyst who opposes renewable energy subsidies, "the higher cost of the electricity from renewable sources and/or the credits that the electric distribution company is forced to pay (instead of the lower cost electricity from traditional sources) is, in one way or another, passed on to electric customers in the form of higher bills for electricity."[10] Environmentalists argue that the price of wind is decreasing and if regulations, such as a cap-and-trade program or a carbon tax, are enacted, wind would become even more cost-competitive with coal. According to the World Wildlife Fund, "even if there was no price on carbon, clean renewable technologies like wind, geothermal power and solid biomass will be cost-competitive with conventional coal by 2030. If, however, the true cost of coal was factored into its price, these sustainable low-carbon technologies would be even cheaper than coal today."[11]

Making Coal Cleaner

Many electric utilities and coal groups think the best government strategy for reducing the electricity sector's contribution to climate change is to invest in clean coal technologies. These groups are concerned about the intermittent nature of wind and solar energy and contend that renewables will never supply enough energy to keep up with U.S. electricity demand. They argue that coal's ability to provide stable relatively inexpensive power, twenty-four hours a day seven days a week, means that it will remain a primary source of electricity for the United States and the world for the foreseeable future. According to the American Coalition for Clean Coal Electricity (ACCCE),

> unlike folks who are saying that reducing greenhouse gases in the utility sector will require us to use different energy sources, we believe that the only way to get that done is to figure out how to use our current energy resources differently. If we don't develop the technology here, it won't make its way to China, India and other places in the developing world that will continue to use massive amounts of coal no matter what we do in the United States. And if we want to solve a global issue such as climate change, China and India must be part of the solution.[12]

The ACCCE maintains that "[clean coal] technology isn't 20 years away—some of it is here today. There have already been technology demonstrations of greenhouse gas emissions control for existing power plants, but more funding is needed to make the technology possible everywhere."[13]

Many environmental groups and others are skeptical that coal can ever be "clean." They maintain "clean coal" is a marketing campaign that holds little promise of actually achieving its goals. According to Greenpeace,

> Clean coal is an attempt by the coal industry to try and make itself relevant in the age of renewables. Existing clean coal technologies do nothing to mitigate the environmental effects of coal mining or the devastating effects of global warming. Coal is the dirtiest fuel there is and belongs in the past. Much higher emission cuts can be made using currently available natural gas, wind and modern biomass that are already in widespread use. Clean, inexpensive. This is where investment

U.S. Department of Energy Promotes Clean Coal Power Plants

More often than not when people are talking about "clean coal" technologies, whether pro or con, they are referring to a certain type of new power plant called an *Integrated Gasification Combined Cycle*, or IGCC, power plant. IGCCs are huge facilities where coal is converted into a gas using common engineering and chemical technologies. This gas, called syngas, is then piped to another area of the facility where it is used to generate electricity. The fact that coal is not burned, but rather "gasified," is an important characteristic of IGCC power plants. It enables easy capture of CO_2 and pollutants, such as nitrogen oxides, sulfur dioxide, and mercury.

Capturing and sequestering CO_2 is a part of the U.S. Department of Energy's plan to reduce CO_2 from electricity generation. The department envisions that CO_2 captured at IGCC plants will be compressed and transported to sites where it will be injected deep underground. Studies have shown that injecting CO_2 into deep geologic formations can permanently sequester it and keep it from entering the atmosphere and contributing to climate change. The Department of Energy is also interested in injecting CO_2 into old oil and natural gas wells to enhance their recovery. So far there are only a handful of IGCC test plants in the United States and a few CO_2 sequestration sites. There are several new IGCC plants with sequestration sites already picked out that are expected to go online in the future, however.

should be directed, rather than squandering valuable resources on a dirty dinosaur.[14]

The ACCCE and Greenpeace may not agree on government investment in clean coal. They do agree on something, however: Neither group is happy with the cap-and-trade legislation, the so-called Waxman-Markey bill, which passed the U.S. House of Representatives in the summer of 2009. The ACCCE contends the legislation's cap and its timeline are too onerous and "could act as a deterrent" to bringing carbon-reducing technologies, such as clean coal, to the marketplace.[15] Greenpeace, on the other hand, believes the legislation "sets emission reduction targets far lower than science demands, then undermines even those targets with massive offsets."[16]

Policy makers' decisions on how to reduce greenhouse gases from the electricity sector are hugely important. Electricity is used to produce virtually every product or good sold or used in the United States. It charges our iPods, our cellular telephones, and our computers. Choosing the best strategy to ensure that electricity is available, but that its impacts to climate change are minimized, is one of the most important decisions facing governments in the United States and around the world.

Notes

1. U.S. Energy Information Administration, *Electric Power Annual: Electric Power Industry 2007: Year in Review*, January 21, 2009. www.eia.doe.gov.
2. U.S. Energy Information Administration, *Electric Power Annual*.
3. U.S. Department of Energy, *20% Wind Energy by 2030*, October 2008. www.20percentwind.org.
4. American Wind Energy Association, "Wind Energy Tax Incentive Wins Extension to End of 2005," news release, September 24, 2004. www.awea.org.
5. Ryan Wiser, "Testimony Prepared for a Hearing on 'Clean Energy: From the Margins to the Mainstream,'" Senate Finance Committee, Thursday, March 29, 2007. http://eetd.lbl.gov.
6. Paul Gipe, "Why I Oppose the Production Tax Credit," Wind-works.org, February 12, 2003. www.wind-works.org.
7. "Summary Map: Renewable Portfolio Standards," Database for State Incentives for Renewables and Efficiency. www.dsireusa.org.
8. Pew Center for Global Climate Change, "Renewable and Alternative Energy Portfolio Standards," updated September 18, 2009. www.pewclimate.org.
9. Matthew Wald, "Cost Works Against Alternative and Renewable Energy Sources in Time of Recession," *New York Times*, March 28, 2009.
10. Glenn Schleede, "'Big Money' Discovers the Huge Tax Breaks and Subsidies for 'Wind Energy' While Taxpayers and Electric Customers Pick Up the Tab," Minnesotans for Sustainability, April 14, 2005. www.mnforsustain.org.
11. World Wildlife Fund, "The Cost of Coal on the Environment," news release, May 4, 2007. www.panda.org.

12. America's Power, "Frequently Asked Questions," 2007–2009. www.americaspower.org.

13. America's Power, "Frequently Asked Questions."

14. Greenpeace, "Unmasking the Truth Behind 'Clean Coal.'" www.greenpeace.org.

15. America's Power, "Legislation We Can Support," 2007–2009. www.americaspower.org.

16. Greenpeace, "Greenpeace Opposes Waxman-Markey," news release, June 25, 2009. www.greenpeace.org.

CHAPTER 8

Reducing Agriculture's Contribution to Global Warming

The U.S. agricultural sector provides food, fiber, fuels, and raw materials for the country and the world. According to the 2007 Census of Agriculture, there were 2.2 million farms, covering an area of 922 million acres (373 million hectares) in the United States.[1] Agriculture is somewhat unique in its ability to both produce and reduce greenhouse gases. According to the U.S. Environmental Protection Agency (EPA), the agricultural sector emitted about 413 million metric tons of greenhouse gases, or 6 percent of the warming emissions in the United States, in 2007.[2] Agriculture, however, also offsets a significant amount of greenhouse gas emissions through carbon sequestration. According to the EPA, the agricultural sector sequestered, or removed from the atmosphere, about 21 million metric tons of greenhouse gases in 2002.[3] The federal government has many programs that encourage farm operators to adopt environmentally friendly farming practices. These programs help lower agriculture's net greenhouse gas emissions.

Agriculture's Potent Warming Emissions

Agricultural operations emit two potent greenhouse gases. Fifty-four percent of agriculture's greenhouse gas emissions come from nitrous oxide (N_2O) emitted primarily from soil as a result

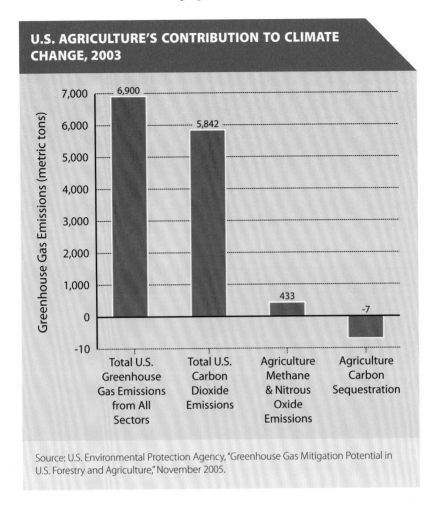

U.S. AGRICULTURE'S CONTRIBUTION TO CLIMATE CHANGE, 2003

Source: U.S. Environmental Protection Agency, "Greenhouse Gas Mitigation Potential in U.S. Forestry and Agriculture," November 2005.

of fertilizer application and other crop management practices.[4] Nitrous oxide is a powerful greenhouse gas. It is about three hundred times more potent than carbon dioxide at warming the earth. Most of the rest of agriculture's greenhouse gas emissions come from methane (CH_4), another potent warming gas. Methane, which is about twenty-five times more potent than carbon dioxide, is emitted directly from cattle, and other ruminant animals, as they digest feed. Cattle vent about 34 percent of agricultural greenhouse gas emissions.[5] Methane is also released from decomposing animal manure. This accounts for about 11 percent of agriculture's greenhouse gas emissions.[6]

Promoting Efficient Fertilizer Use

The use of fertilizers is a major source of agricultural greenhouse gas emissions. Farmers spread commercial fertilizers or manure on land to ensure their crops have nitrogen, phosphorus, potassium, and other nutrients that are necessary for plant growth. If any of these are missing or hard to obtain from the soil, crop growth will be limited. However, too much of these nutrients, particularly nitrogen and phosphorus, creates water and air pollution and greenhouse gas emissions. Excess nitrogen is converted into a powerful warming gas, nitrous oxide, which is then emitted into the atmosphere.

The underlying concept in reducing nitrous oxide emissions is to encourage efficient fertilizer use. By using soil testing and other processes, farmers can determine how much fertilizer they need and apply only what is necessary for plant growth. According to the Intergovernmental Panel on Climate Change, efficient fertilizer use can reduce agriculture's nitrous oxide emissions by about 17 percent.[7]

A long-standing government conservation program encourages farmers to use fertilizer more efficiently. The Natural Resources Conservation Service, an agency of the U.S. Department of Agriculture, has been around since the 1930s (it used to be known as the Soil Conservation Service). It promotes and helps farmers to implement a wide range of conservation practices including "nutrient management plans." Nutrient management is a process used by farmers to manage the amount, form, placement, and timing of land application of fertilizer or manure to protect against their adverse impacts. Nutrient management plans entail soil testing, manure testing, erosion control practices, and timing of fertilizer and manure application.

The primary objectives of many of these measures are usually not related solely to climate change issues, but rather to such aims as reducing environmental pollution and natural resource degradation. However, nutrient management plans and other conservation practices can reduce agriculture's overall greenhouse gas emissions.

Cattle Are a Major Methane Source

Globally, ruminant livestock such as cattle, goats, and sheep are the largest source of human-related methane and the third largest source in the United States. Ruminants' digestive systems entail the use of two stomachs and a process called enteric fermentation, which allows them to obtain nutrition from grasses and woody plants that other animals cannot digest. Enteric fermentation allows ruminant animals to live off grasses and hay but it also produces a lot of methane.

Cattle are the biggest producers of agricultural methane emissions. An adult cow emits anywhere from 175 to 250 pounds (79 to 113 kilograms) of methane each day, by burping, exhaling, or flatulence.[8] As there are about 100 million cattle in the United States and 1.3 billion globally, cattle methane emissions add up to significant amounts. The EPA estimates that cattle emit about 5.5 million metric tons of methane per year into the atmosphere and account for 20 percent of U.S. methane emissions.[9]

According to the EPA, "the most promising approach for reducing methane emissions from U.S. livestock is to improve the quality of forage (the grasses and plants cows eat) and cattle feed."[10] Researchers have found that cattle which are fed diets high in grain and low in fiber produce more meat and milk than cattle fed other kinds of diets. The more meat and milk each cow produces means fewer cows are needed to supply the beef and dairy products humans consume. Fewer cows means less methane emissions. Additionally, high-grain low-fiber diets spend less time in the cow's rumen where enteric fermentation takes place, and this leads to fewer methane emissions per cow. In addition to high-grain diets, researchers are looking for other ways to reduce cattle's methane emissions. In a 2009 story in the *New*

York Times, Erin Fitzgerald, a consultant for the American dairy industry states, "the industry wants to avert the possibility that customers will equate dairies with, say, coal plants."[11] According to Fitzgerald, the dairy industry has started a "cow of the future" program, looking for ways to reduce methane emissions from cows by 25 percent.[12] According to Colorado State University scientist William Wailes, who is working on the cow of the future, "scientists are looking at everything from genetics—cows that naturally belch less—to adjusting the bacteria in the cow's stomach."[13]

The federal Ruminant Livestock Efficiency Program also aims to help farmers reduce livestock methane emissions. President George H.W. Bush established the program in 1993 as part of his United States Climate Change Action Plan. The program educates farmers on ways to improve cattle forage and encour-

A California dairy farmer stands near a pile of manure, which is a byproduct of the methane digester he has installed. The equipment transforms detrimental agricultural gases from cows into usable energy. AP Images.

ages improved livestock efficiency as a way of reducing methane emissions.

Making Energy out of Manure

Managing manure—according to the EPA, a single dairy cow produces 120 pounds (54 kg) of wet manure a day—is an important issue for agricultural operations.[14] Smaller farms, which grow crops and raise animals, can usually recycle all their manure by applying it to their fields. Large livestock operations would need thousands of acres to recycle all their manure, however, so instead they end up storing it in onsite ponds, lagoons, or tanks. Most livestock operations use water to move manure from place to place. The storage of huge amounts of liquid manure creates anaerobic (without oxygen) conditions that lead to the production and release of methane into the atmosphere.

"Agriculture can answer the challenge of climate change while feeding a troubled and hungry world."

In the late 1990s, the U.S. federal government began an initiative to promote the use of manure for energy production as a way to reduce greenhouse gas emissions. The AgSTAR program, created by the EPA, the Department of Agriculture, and the Department of Energy, encourages farm operators to install methane digesters. Methane digesters are huge vessels wherein microbes degrade manure, as they would in a storage lagoon or tank, except the methane is captured and used to produce electricity, heat, or hot water. Methane digesters can reduce methane emissions, as well as odors and pathogens from manure. Additionally, energy produced from methane digesters displaces fossil-fuel energy generation and avoids its greenhouse gas emissions. The AgSTAR program provides resources, educational information, and technical assistance to farmers looking to in-

An International Methane Reduction Partnership

Climate change is a serious environmental challenge that requires a global response. Methane is a potent greenhouse gas (GHG), second only to carbon dioxide in its contribution to climate change. It is of particular strategic importance given its atmospheric properties and the suite of currently available, cost-effective reduction options. As such, focusing mitigation efforts on methane can yield near-term climate impacts along with major economic, air quality, and energy benefits.

The United States and 13 other countries formed the Methane to Markets Partnership in 2004. The goal of the Partnership is to help reduce methane emissions quickly and cost-effectively through a collaborative, multilateral framework that unites public and private interests to fight climate change by advancing the recovery and use of methane as a clean energy source. By engaging public and private sector parties, Methane to Markets brings together the technical and market expertise, financing, and technology necessary for methane capture and use project development.

The Partnership focuses on developing projects in four major methane emissions source areas: agriculture, coal mines, landfills, and oil and gas systems. In each of these sectors, cost-effective methane emission reduction technologies and practices are currently available to

stall methane digesters. The program also helps farmers identify funding sources, such as state tax credits and grants, to help offset the costs of installing methane digesters.

Many states consider methane digesters a source of renewable energy and encourage their installation. One study found that if all U.S. livestock manure were put inside methane digesters, approximately 90 billion kilowatt-hours of electricity would be produced, which is enough to power millions of houses.[15] The study also found that by generating power with manure instead of fos-

capture and use the methane gas as a fuel for electricity generation, on-site energy needs, or off-site gas sales. However, despite the availability of proven technologies and the understanding of associated environmental and financial benefits, methane recovery and use projects are not yet the global norm. In many countries, financial, institutional, informational, regulatory, and other barriers have impeded the adoption of methane recovery technologies. Methane to Markets is working to identify and address these barriers in order to combat climate change and deliver clean energy to markets all around the world. . . .

Methane to Markets in Vietnam In Vietnam, swine farmers are recovering methane through household, farm, multiple-family, and communal demonstration systems. Many of these projects use recovered gas for cooking fuel, reducing the harmful health impacts of cooking with wood fuels by improving air quality in enclosed kitchen spaces. For example, in northern Vietnam's Tu Duong village, communal project participants collect pig wastes from 100 family-owned backyard piggeries. The waste is transferred through a gravity-based village canal system to a series of anaerobic digesters. The gas is piped back to the families and used as cooking and lighting fuel. The fee charged for the gas pays for system maintenance and a full-time operator.

SOURCE: Environmental Protection Agency, *The U.S. Government's Methane to Markets Partnership Accomplishments; Fourth Annual Report*, October 2009. www.epa.gov.

sil fuels, approximately 4 percent of U.S. electricity sector greenhouse gas emissions could be eliminated.[16] Most states that have renewable portfolio standard programs, which require electric utilities to provide a certain percentage of renewable electricity to their customers, as discussed in Chapter 7, consider methane digesters a source of renewable energy. In these states, farmers can use the digesters to meet their own electricity needs and sell the excess to the local electric utility. Utilities in states that have renewable portfolio standard programs will generally pay more for electricity from methane digesters than utilities in states without such programs.

Agriculture as a Solution to Climate Change

In a speech in 2003, U.S. Senator Pat Roberts from Kansas asserted that "agriculture can answer the challenge of climate change while feeding a troubled and hungry world."[17] His remarks refer to the fact that agricultural land can soak up carbon dioxide and reduce its level in the atmosphere in a process referred to as carbon sequestration. The U.S. Department of Agriculture has estimated that "farm and grazing land soils store about 20 million metric tons of carbon a year and could store an additional 180 million metric tons annually."[18]

The Natural Resources Conservation Service, which promotes efficient fertilizer use and other environmentally friendly practices, also promotes a farming practice called conservation tillage, which can increase the amount of carbon sequestered on agricultural lands. Tillage is the practice of plowing soil, seeds, and residues from previous crops into a field before replanting it. Traditional tillage practices typically cause soil erosion problems and reduce the amount of carbon that soils can sequester. In conservation tillage, at least 30 percent of crop residues are left as is on the soil. Doing so disturbs the soil less, and therefore allows soil to accumulate carbon and keep it out of the atmosphere. Using conservation tillage practices can also avoid fossil fuel greenhouse gas emissions because less farm equipment is used and there are fewer trips to the field. According to Kris Brye, a researcher for the University of Arkansas System's Division of Agriculture, "We can't do anything about the climate, but by adopting conservation tillage practices, we can increase carbon sequestration and storage capacity."[19]

Agriculture can also play a role in reducing carbon emissions from the transportation sector. A significant amount of U.S. corn is currently used to produce ethanol to make E85 fuel for use in flex fuel vehicles. Soybean crops are used to produce an environmentally friendly form of diesel called biodiesel. To the extent these fuels can supplant petroleum-produced gasoline and diesel fuel they can help reduce greenhouse gas emissions from the transportation sector. The federal government promotes the production and use of ethanol and biodiesel through a range of policies, including tax credits and the Renewable Fuel Standard, which requires the nation's supply of transportation fuel to contain a certain portion of renewable fuels, discussed in Chapter 5.

Despite the government's support of biofuels, the use of corn to produce fuel is a concern to United Nations Food and Agriculture Organization, anti-hunger groups, and some scientists. They contend ethanol will not slow climate change, and they express concern that farmers may start to grow crops meant for biofuel production rather than the ones that can be used as food. In *Time* magazine in 2008, reporter Michael Grunwald writes, "several new studies show the biofuel boom is doing exactly the opposite of what its proponents intended: it's dramatically accelerating global warming, imperiling the planet in the name of saving it. Meanwhile, by diverting grain and oilseed crops from dinner plates to fuel tanks, biofuels are jacking up world food prices and endangering the hungry."[20] The Renewable Fuels Association counters that ethanol reduces greenhouse gas emissions when compared to gasoline and there is a sufficient supply of corn for both food and fuel. According to the association, "exaggerated claims about the threats [of ethanol fuel] to engines, the environment, food supply, and the economy simply don't pass muster.[21]

Increasing the use of biofuels is not the only climate change policy that causes concern about food prices. Some farmers and conservative lawmakers think that food prices will increase if the country enacts comprehensive climate change legislation, such as the Waxman-Markey bill, which would establish a national carbon dioxide cap-and-trade program. Conservative groups such as the Heritage Foundation, which are skeptical about climate change to begin with, believe that the economic vitality of the agricultural sector will be damaged by a cap-and-trade program and food prices will increase. According to the Heritage Foundation, "Waxman-Markey's effect on farmers should raise a red flag for those in the farm belt and will put U.S. agriculture at a tremendous competitive disadvantage if enacted. Consumers will feel the pain as well, not only from the increase in their own energy prices, but increased food prices. And for what? A change in the temperature too small to notice."[22] Other groups, however, have found that the agricultural sector may benefit under a cap-and-trade program. A University of Tennessee report commissioned by the 25×'25 group, which promotes renewable energy, found that the agriculture and forestry sectors could see an additional $13 billion in revenues under a "properly constructed" cap-and-trade program.[23] The increased revenues would primarily come from selling carbon credits based on a farm's ability to sequester carbon. Speaking to a reporter from the *Kansas City Star*, Ernie Shea of 25×'25 said, "We're not saying this is a huge cash cow for the farmers in this country. We don't see a collapse, either. We see a slight bump."[24]

Agriculture has typically enjoyed less government regulation than other economic sectors because of its unique role in the history of the country and because it produces a vital commodity. Government efforts to reduce agriculture's impact on climate change ultimately must consider the effect of these policies on the availability of food in the United States and the world.

Notes

1. U.S. Department of Agriculture, *2007 Agriculture Census*, February 2009. www.agcensus.usda.gov.
2. U.S. Environmental Protection Agency, *Inventory of U.S. Greenhouse Gas Emissions and Sinks: 1990–2007*, April 2009. www.epa.gov.
3. U.S. Environmental Protection Agency, *Inventory of U.S. Greenhouse Gas Emissions and Sinks: 1990–2002*, April 2004.
4. EPA, *Inventory of U.S. Greenhouse Gas*, April 2009.
5. EPA, *Inventory of U.S. Greenhouse Gas*, April 2009.

6. EPA, *Inventory of U.S. Greenhouse Gas*, April 2009.
7. Intergovernmental Panel on Climate Change, *Technologies, Policies and Measures for Mitigating Climate Change*, November 1996. www.gcrio.org.
8. U.S. Environmental Protection Agency, "Ruminant Livestock: Frequent Questions," March 21, 2007. www.epa.gov.
9. EPA, "Ruminant Livestock."
10. EPA, "Ruminant Livestock."
11. Quoted in Leslie Kaufman, "Greening the Herds: A New Diet to Cap Gas," *New York Times*, June 4, 2009.
12. Kaufman, "Greening the Herds: A New Diet to Cap Gas."
13. Quoted in Kaufman, "Greening the Herds: A New Diet to Cap Gas."
14. U.S. Environmental Protection Agency, Region 9, "Animal Waste: What's the Problem," updated July 10, 2009. www.epa.gov.
15. Amanda Cuéllar and Michael Webber, "Cow Power: the Energy and Emissions Benefits of Converting Manure to Biogas," *Environmental Research Letters*, July 24, 2008.
16. Cuéllar and Webber, "Cow Power," *Environmental Research Letters*.
17. Pat Roberts, "Remarks at USDA Carbon Sequestration Event," Wyandotte, Kansas, Agriculture Hall of Fame, June 6, 2003. http://roberts.senate.gov.
18. "Los Alamos Lab Technology Measures Carbon Dioxide in Soil with Millimeter Precision; Method Gauges Use of Farmland as 'Carbon Sink' to Help Reduce Greenhouse Gas," AScribe Newswire, May 29, 2002.
19. University of Arkansas Division of Agriculture, "Carbon Credits May Offer Farmers New Income Source," http://arkansasagnews.uark.edu.
20. Michael Grunwald, "The Clean Energy Scam," *Time*, March 27, 2008. www.time.com.
21. Renewable Fuel Association, "New Tactics, Same Tired Playbook: Ethanol Critics Repackage Same Misinformation in New Pro-Oil Campaign." www.ethanolrfa.org.
22. Heritage Foundation, "For Farmers Cap and Trade Is Permanent Drought Season," *The Foundry*, June 9, 2009. http://blog.heritage.org.
23. Daniel de la Torre Ugarte et al., *Analysis of the Implications of Climate Change and Energy Legislation to the Agricultural Sector*, 20×'25 [organization], November 2009.
24. Quoted in Scott Canon, "Farming Could Benefit Under Cap-and-Trade, Report Says," *Kansas City Star*, November 11, 2009. www.kansascity.com.

CHAPTER 9

Forests and Land Use

If it were not for the forests and the ocean, the earth would be significantly warmer, and humans and other animals would not be able to survive. Trees are the largest photosynthesizing units on earth. They absorb massive amounts of carbon dioxide, help cool the earth, and supply oxygen, which is vital for life. Russia contains more forested land than any other country, with nearly 2 billion acres (809 million hectares) of mostly boreal forest. The country with the second-largest forested area is Brazil, with nearly 1.2 billion acres (486 million hectares) of tropical forests. Canada and the United States are third and fourth with about 770 million acres and 750 million acres (312 million hectares and 304 million hectares), respectively, of boreal and temperate forests. It is estimated that the earth's forests cover nearly 10 billion acres (4 billion hectares), or 30 percent of the planet's land area.

Forests Can Absorb and Release Carbon Dioxide

Forests play an important role in mitigating climate change. All the forests of the world are carbon sinks, soaking up huge quantities of carbon dioxide from the atmosphere and storing it in the form of woody biomass. It is estimated that the forests of the world store 283 billion metric tons of carbon.[1] In 2009, researchers from the University of Leeds found that each year tropical forests absorb enough carbon dioxide to offset the emissions from the world's cars and trucks. According to Simon Lewis, lead researcher of the study, "we are receiving a free subsidy from nature. Tropical forest trees are absorbing about 18 percent of the carbon dioxide added to the atmosphere each year from burning fossil fuels, substantially buffering the rate of climate change."[2]

When forests are removed, the climate suffers a double whammy. First, the carbon-storing capacity of the forest is removed, so the earth's ability to buffer or mitigate climate change is decreased. Second, the carbon that was once stored in the forest typically ends up being released into the air through burning or decomposing matter. As a result, what was once a carbon sink becomes a carbon source. Deforestation accounts for 12 to 20 percent of the human-caused greenhouse gas emissions in the world.[3]

Deforestation

Forest losses occur throughout the world mostly because of deforestation, where forests are cleared by people to obtain wood, or where the forest is simply destroyed so the land can be converted to agricultural fields or roads. Natural events such as lightning-caused forest fires also destroy forests. During the period from 2000 to 2005, it is estimated that the world lost about 32 million acres (13 million hectares) of forest per year—or thirty-six football fields of forest per minute—mostly through human-caused deforestation.[4] The greatest amount of deforestation occurs in the tropical forests of South America and Africa. During 2000 to 2005, these forests lost about 21 million acres, or nearly two thirds of the planet's entire forest loss.[5] Forest losses occur throughout the world, however. North America lost nearly 900,000 acres (364,000 hectares) of forestland during this time.[6]

Climate change concerns, among other concerns such as loss of habitat, have led to government efforts to protect forestland around the world. Preventing deforestation in tropical regions has been a long-standing goal of many environmental and social organizations. Groups such as the Rainforest Action Network and the Tropical Rainforest Coalition were formed in the 1980s and 1990s to alert the world to the dramatic losses of tropical forests that were occurring and to prevent them. As governments have looked for ways to mitigate climate change, they too have recognized the importance of protecting forests. Governments are incorporating forest protection and land use policies into their overall strategy to reduce climate change.

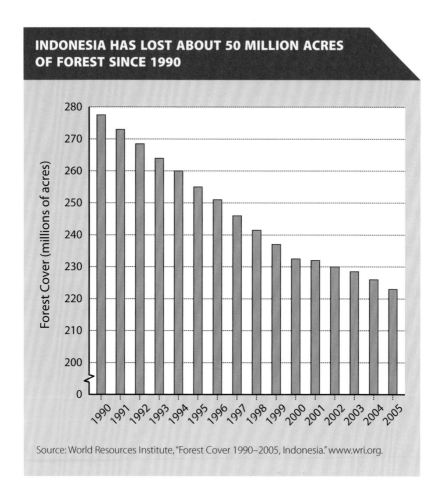

INDONESIA HAS LOST ABOUT 50 MILLION ACRES OF FOREST SINCE 1990

Source: World Resources Institute, "Forest Cover 1990–2005, Indonesia." www.wri.org.

During the period from 2000 to 2005, it is estimated that the world lost about 32 million acres of forest per year— or thirty-six football fields of forest per minute—mostly through human-caused deforestation.

Avoiding Deforestation as Climate Change Strategy

The United Nations Framework Convention on Climate Change (UNFCCC) and the Kyoto Protocol recognize activities that increase forestation as important for climate change mitigation. However, they generally do not recognize the prevention of deforestation as a climate change mitigation technique. Developed countries that signed the Kyoto Protocol, such as Japan, Russia, and the countries of the European Union, agreed to reduce their emissions of greenhouse gases to specific levels. These countries can get credit for emissions reductions by funding projects in developing countries that increase forestation. The idea is that conversion of nonforested land into forestland can absorb and offset other greenhouse gas emission. However, in 1997, when the Kyoto Protocol was being drawn up, government negotiators rejected provisions to give credit to projects that protected established forests or avoided deforestation. There were two primary reasons for the rejection. First, the Kyoto Protocol negotiators believed there was too much uncertainty in how much carbon was actually stored in a forest. Second, many of them did not think countries should get credit for forests that were already established because the country did not really do anything to create the forest.

When world leaders met in Copenhagen, Denmark, in December 2009 to try to create a new international climate change treaty, the issue of whether to give credits to projects that avoid deforestation was again debated. Generally, the issue of uncertainty surrounding how much carbon a forest can actually store

The Copenhagen Accord Recognizes the Role of Avoided Deforestation

... 6. We recognize the crucial role of reducing emission from deforestation and forest degradation and the need to enhance removal of greenhouse gas emission by forests and agree on the need to provide positive incentives to such actions through the immediate establishment of a mechanism including REDD-plus [reducing emissions from deforestation or degredation], to enable the mobilization of financial resources from developed countries.

7. We decide to pursue various approaches, including opportunities to use markets, to enhance the cost-effectiveness of, and to promote mitigation actions. Developing countries, especially those with low-emitting economies, should be provided incentives to continue to develop on a low-emission pathway.

8. Scaled up, new and additional, predictable and adequate funding as well as improved access shall be provided to developing countries, in accordance with the relevant provisions of the Convention, to enable and support enhanced action on mitigation, including substantial finance to reduce emissions from deforestation and forest degradation (REDD-plus), adaptation, technol-

has been addressed. Researchers from around the world have developed methods to quantify the amount of carbon contained in various forests. In 2009, several published reports quantified the amount of carbon contained in tropical, boreal (northern forests of Canada, Russia, and Scandinavia), and temperate forests.

Upon the issue of whether countries deserve credit for their established forests, there is still much debate. Organizations such as the Nature Conservancy contend that avoided deforestation should be recognized as a climate change mitigation technique. They argue that if countries can obtain credits, which can be sold in the international carbon market, they will be more likely to

ogy development and transfer and capacity-building, for enhanced implementation of the Convention. The collective commitment by developed countries is to provide new and additional resources, including forestry and investments through international institutions, approaching USD 30 billion for the period 2010–2012 with balanced allocation between adaptation and mitigation. Funding for adaptation will be prioritized for the most vulnerable developing countries, such as the least developed countries, small islands, developing States and Africa. In the context of meaningful mitigation actions and transparency on implementation, developed countries commit to a goal of mobilizing jointly USD 100 billion dollars a year by 2020 to address the needs of developing countries. This funding will come from a wide variety of sources, public and private, bilateral and multilateral, including alternative sources of finance. New multilateral funding for adaptation will be delivered through effective and efficient fund arrangements, with a governance structure providing for equal representation of developed and developing countries. A significant portion of such funding should flow through the Copenhagen Green Climate Fund. . . .

SOURCE: **Copenhagen Accord (Advance unedited version Decision-/CP.15), December 18, 2009.**

adopt policies that protect their forest resources. In 1996, the Nature Conservancy forged a partnership with the Bolivian government and a Bolivian environmental organization, Fundación Amigos de la Naturaleza, to demonstrate the value of avoided deforestation in climate change strategies. The groups solicited funds from energy companies to buy a 2-million-acre tract of Bolivian forestland that was slated for logging. The energy

---

Following pages: About 32 million acres of forest were cleared every year between 2000 and 2005. Most deforestation, such as this clearing project in Brazil, takes place in South America and Africa. Antonio Scorza/AFP/Getty Images.

companies that put up the funding are betting that avoided deforestation projects will be eligible for climate change credits, whether through an international treaty, voluntary markets, or through national or regional climate change cap-and-trade programs. The 2 million acres (809,000 hectares) of forestland became a part of the Noel Kempff Mercado National Forest, bringing its total protected forestland from 1.9 million (769,000 hectares) to 3.9 million acres (1.6 million hectares). The Nature Conservancy says that the Noel Kempff Climate Action Project, as it is called, is expected to avoid or mitigate the release of up to 5.8 million tons of carbon dioxide into the atmosphere over thirty years by preventing logging and agricultural conversion of the land.[7] According to the Nature Conservancy's Greg Fishbein, "forest protection is now seen as one of the most powerful and cost-effective tools we have to combat climate change. This is a tremendous opportunity to create monetary value in standing forests through carbon markets."[8]

Many other groups, such as Greenpeace International, oppose giving credit to countries for reduced deforestation, however. One argument against the offset credits, as they are called, is that they will depress the need for other industries to reduce their greenhouse gas emissions. Greenpeace has warned that a widespread allotment of forest offset credits will depress the price of carbon in carbon markets as much as 75 percent, and therefore remove the incentive for polluters to reduce carbon emissions.[9] According to Damon Moglen of Greenpeace, credits for avoided deforestation are a "get out of jail free card." He states "by using offsets, industry will be able to sidestep emissions reductions."[10]

Many indigenous people also oppose giving credits for "reducing emissions from deforestation or degradation," or REDD, as the policy has become known. The Indigenous Environmental Network thinks REDD policies are wrong for many reasons. It maintains REDD policies violate the rights of indigenous people and are merely a front for large international companies to buy a stake in forests. Additionally, the network does not agree that

REDD policies will protect forestland or mitigate climate change. According to Tom B.K. Goldtooth, the executive director of the Indigenous Environmental Network,

> REDD proposals are largely opposed by many Indigenous Peoples, not all, but most. To be involved with a system that defines something that we hold sacred, and that is the sacred element of air, to be part of a neo-colonial system that privatizes the atmosphere, to put a money value to it, creates resistance from our heart. It is a modern world that capitalizes everything, that puts a monetary value to life itself, it is about ownership of life, it is about disrespecting life. I call it a corruption of the sacred, that's what carbon forest offsets within REDD is."[11]

The agreement reached in Copenhagen in 2009, called the Copenhagen Accord, recognized the role of REDD toward mitigating climate change but left many details unresolved and many debates still continuing. The accord suggests that avoided deforestation is a legitimate climate change reduction technique. Additionally, developed countries pledged billions of dollars in initial funding to help developing countries preserve their forestlands and reduce deforestation activities. The text of the accord refers several times to safeguarding indigenous peoples' rights. This language has eased the concerns of some indigenous people. The accord left unanswered the question of whether avoided deforestation projects would receive offset credits under a carbon trading scheme, however. This question will likely remain at the center of future negotiations on REDD policies. According to Kate Dooley from the European forest protection organization called FERN (Forests and the European Union Resource Network), "the biggest [obstacle] to a fruitful REDD debate is the underlying assumption that REDD will eventually be financed through carbon offsets or some comparable form of tradable emission unit." According to Dooley, this question represents "a substantial deadlock which the 'expert' level negotiators are unlikely to be able to resolve due to fundamental differences in each country's approach to and interpretations of what REDD is."[12]

The debate over whether to include credits for projects that avoid deforestation in tropical regions is also being waged in the United States. The Waxman-Markey cap-and-trade legislation from the U.S. House of Representatives includes provisions that would allow American companies to receive credits toward meeting the carbon cap by funding projects in other countries that avoid deforestation. Additionally, companies that are required to reduce carbon emissions under the California Global Warming Solutions Act of 2006 will be able to obtain credits for funding tropical avoided-deforestation projects.

State and Local Land-Use Policies as Climate Change Tools

Saving entire forests is not the only strategy governments are using to combat climate change. Many people think small-scale land-use changes can affect climate change. They believe that the removal of green cover, in general, has contributed to warming the earth, and not just through reducing green plants' and trees' ability to sequester carbon dioxide. According to Georgia Tech professor Brian Stone, "across the U.S. as a whole, approximately 50 percent of the warming that has occurred since 1950 is due to land-use changes (usually in the form of clearing forest for crops or cities) rather than to the emission of greenhouse gases. Most large U.S. cities, including Atlanta, are warming at more than twice the rate of the planet as a whole—a rate that is mostly attributable to land-use change."[13] A study out of Purdue University seems to support Stone's contention. Researchers at Purdue found that increased local temperatures can partially be explained by local land-use changes from greener to less green covers.[14] The researchers concluded that local and regional strategies, such as creating green spaces and buffer zones in and around urban areas, could be a tool in addressing climate change.

According to Stone, "as we look to address the climate change issue from a land-use perspective, there is a huge opportunity for local and state governments."[15]

Many states promote or require that municipal land-use plans recognize climate change. The New York Department of Environmental Conservation developed a "smart community pledge" that has been adopted by dozens of New York state communities. The communities pledge to keep development resilient to climatic change and to update land-use policies, building codes, and community plans in ways that reduce sprawl, minimize development in floodplains, and protect forests. The Massachusetts Smart Growth Open Space Residential Bylaw requires that at least 50 percent of the land in residential developments be conserved. Additionally, open space is required to be legally protected and grouped in contiguous tracts. Georgia and Wisconsin have also developed similar regulations.

In 2007, the state of Washington enacted legislation creating a Transfer of Development Rights (TDR) program to address climate change. A TDR program is a market-based mechanism that encourages the voluntary transfer of growth from places where a community would like to see less development, referred to as sending areas, to places where a community would like to see more development, referred to as receiving areas. The program focuses on the conservation of rural, agricultural, and forested lands. After development rights are successfully transferred from undeveloped parcels to urban areas, a permanent easement or deed restriction is placed on the undeveloped property to prohibit future development. A number of state and local governments have cited TDR programs as a useful tool for addressing the causes of climate change.

Although the approaches may vary, most people agree that forestry and land use are vital components of any climate change strategy. In its report *Mitigating Climate Change Through Food and Land Use*, the Worldwatch Institute writes that "no strategy for mitigating global climate change can be complete or successful without reducing emissions from agriculture, forestry, and other land uses."[16]

Notes

1. Food and Agrigulture Organization of the United Nations, *Global Forest Resources Assessment 2005: Progress Towards Sustainable Forest Management*, 2006.
2. Simon Lewis, "One-Fifth of Fossil-Fuel Emissions Absorbed by Threatened Forests," EurekAlert, February 18, 2009. www.eurekalert.org.
3. G.R. van der Werf et al., "CO_2 Emissions from Forest Loss," *Nature Geoscience*, November 1, 2009.
4. FAO, *Global Forest Resources Assessment 2005*.
5. FAO, *Global Forest Resources Assessment 2005*.
6. FAO, *Global Forest Resources Assessment 2005*.
7. Jane Braxton Little, "Carbon Equation," *Nature Conservancy Magazine*, Winter 2009.
8. Quoted in Little, "Carbon Equation."
9. Ben Block, "Climate Debate Focuses on Deforestation," Worldwatch Institute, April 16, 2009.
10. Quoted in Ed Stoddard, "U.S. Carbon Market: Many Projects, Many Clouds," Reuters, August 6, 2009.
11. Indigenous Environmental Network, "The REDD Train Is Going Pretty Fast and It's Left Us at the Station: Interview with Tom B.K. Goldtooth," December 2008. www.ienearth.org.
12. Kate Dooley, "Forest Watch Special Report—UNFCCC Climate Talks, December 7–18, 2009," *EU Forest Watch*, January 2010.
13. Quoted in *Science Daily*, "Reducing Greenhouse Gases May Not Be Enough to Slow Climate Change," November 11, 2009. www.sciencedaily.com.
14. Purdue University, "Study Gives Clearer Picture of How Land-Use Changes Affect U.S. Climate," news release, November 2, 2009. www.purdue.edu.
15. Quoted in *Science Daily*, "Reducing Greenhouse Gases May Not Be Enough to Slow Climate Change," November 11, 2009. www.sciencedaily.com.
16. Sara J. Scherr and Sajal Sthapit, *Mitigating Climate Change Through Food and Land Use*, Washington, DC: Worldwatch Institute, 2008.

CHAPTER 10

Moving Away from the Carbon Economy

Fossil fuels made of carbon have prospered since the beginning of the industrial age. The steam engine fueled with coal propelled the shift to an industrially based society in the eighteenth and nineteenth centuries. With the advent of the gasoline-powered automobile in the twentieth century and the use of natural gas to produce fertilizers and other products, the role of carbon as the prime mover of the world's economy was solidified. More than one hundred years later, fossil fuels are still the most important source of electricity, heat, raw materials, and power for automobiles and trucks.

Three factors lead many experts to surmise that carbon's reign as king of the world's economy is coming to an end. First, fossil fuel supplies are finite and one day, perhaps sooner rather than later in the case of oil, the world will run out of carbonaceous fuels. Second, much of the world's oil supplies are located in politically unstable regions of the world, sometimes causing widely fluctuating price swings for gasoline and diesel fuels. Third, and perhaps most importantly in regard to climate change discussions, all fossil fuels emit carbon dioxide, which scientists say is the primary reason the earth is warming. Speaking to the U.S. Green Building Conference in 2007, former president Bill Clinton said, "it's not going to be easy, but we have to move away from the carbon economy."[1] But what could the economy move to? Many economists, energy analysts, and policy makers think hydrogen or biomass could be the answer to decarbonizing the economy.

"The third Industrial Revolution is the end-game that takes the world out of the old carbon and uranium-based [nuclear] energies and into a non-polluting, sustainable future for the human race."

The Hydrogen Economy

Author and economist Jeremy Rifkin believes hydrogen can replace carbon as the fuel the economy runs on. In 2003, Rifkin published *The Hydrogen Economy: The Creation of the Worldwide Energy Web and the Redistribution of Power on Earth*, in which he makes a case for why he believes we are on the cusp of a new industrial revolution. Rifkin thinks a new hydrogen-powered economy is going to fundamentally change the nature of the global marketplace. In Rifkin's new economy, hydrogen produced using renewable sources, such as wind, solar, and biomass, will provide electricity, heat, and energy for transportation. Rifkin also envisions that, instead of large centralized power plants sending out electricity to tens of thousands of homes, smaller, decentralized hydrogen-fueled sources will generate electricity for a single home or a neighborhood. According to Rifkin, "the third Industrial Revolution is the end-game that takes the world out of the old carbon and uranium-based [nuclear] energies and into a non-polluting, sustainable future for the human race."[2]

Hydrogen fuel cells are the cornerstone of a hydrogen economy. Anything that requires power, such as an automobile, a building, or a computer, can get that power from a fuel cell. Belying their futuristic aura, fuel cells are based on a very old and simple chemical process called electrolysis. In electrolysis, water molecules (H_2O) are split into hydrogen (H_2) and oxygen (O_2) by an electric current. In 1839, William Grove reversed the process of electrolysis for the first time. Using oxygen from the air and hydrogen, he generated electricity and water, thereby creating the first fuel cell. Hydrogen fuel cells generate electricity without the release of carbon dioxide or any other emissions. Their only byproduct is water. This cleanliness makes them very attractive for a climate-friendly decarbonized economy.

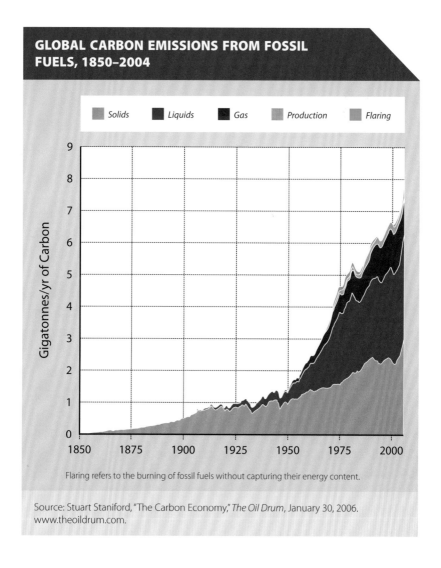

GLOBAL CARBON EMISSIONS FROM FOSSIL FUELS, 1850–2004

Solids   Liquids   Gas   Production   Flaring

Gigatonnes/yr of Carbon

Flaring refers to the burning of fossil fuels without capturing their energy content.

Source: Stuart Staniford, "The Carbon Economy," *The Oil Drum*, January 30, 2006. www.theoildrum.com.

A hydrogen-propelled bus sits outside of the Federal Environment Ministry in Berlin, Germany. John MacDougall/AFP/Getty Images.

The Importance of Renewable Energy

Fuel cells hold great promise as an alternative to fossil fuels, but obtaining hydrogen gas to fuel them is a challenge. Hydrogen gas is the most abundant chemical in the universe—it is the main component of stars like our sun; because it so much lighter than air, however, hydrogen gas does not exist naturally on Earth. Hydrogen is always found combined with other elements, such as with oxygen in water (H_2O) or with carbon in methane (CH_4) or other organic compounds. Scientists have found various ways of extracting hydrogen from these other elements and creating hydrogen gas. All these methods require energy, however. For instance, the process of electrolysis, described above, is commonly used. Because generating hydrogen requires energy, hydrogen fuel cells are not considered a primary energy source. They are considered a carrier of energy or a form of stored energy. In a future hydrogen economy, renewable energy sources, like wind and solar energy, would probably play a key role in producing hydrogen for fuel cells. Turbines placed in windy locations capture the energy in moving wind and convert it into electricity without any greenhouse gas or other emissions. Similarly, sunlight is converted into electricity without any greenhouse gas emissions by using photovoltaic panels placed atop houses or other buildings. In a future hydrogen economy—where emission-free sources are key—electricity would be created from the wind and sun, and this electricity would be used to produce hydrogen for fuel cells. The energy stored in the fuel cells could be released to create electricity to power homes and businesses when the wind is not blowing or the sun is not shining. Alternatively, the hydrogen could be used to power fuel cell vehicles. In this way automobiles would also no longer have tailpipe emissions and such vehicles would depend ultimately on electricity from the sun and wind.

Government efforts to promote renewable energy, such as wind and solar, are viewed by many experts as important for the creation of a hydrogen economy. The federal government has enacted tax credits to make renewable energy more attractive to investors. State and local governments have enacted renewable portfolio standard programs, which require that a certain portion of electricity come from renewable energy sources. These and other government actions to increase the deployment of renewable energy across the country are described in detail in Chapter 7.

One of the major challenges to creating a hydrogen economy is infrastructure. Carbonaceous fuels are trucked, railed, shipped, and piped to power plants, homes, and fueling stations. Hydrogen is a diffuse gas requiring extensive compression before it can be handled, however. This makes trucks and trains generally impractical for transporting it. Pipelines would be suitable, but current pipelines are made for natural gas and would require extensive reworking to handle hydrogen. Many countries and several U.S. states, most notably California, are focusing on building a hydrogen infrastructure in the transportation sector as a starting point for a hydrogen economy.

The California Hydrogen Highway

In 2004, California governor Arnold Schwarzenegger issued an executive order requiring the state to develop a plan to rapidly transition to a hydrogen economy. Schwarzenegger said a hydrogen economy will lead to the lowest possible emissions of greenhouse gases and help mitigate global climate change.[3] The executive order called for the construction of a network of hydrogen fueling stations along California's major highways by 2010. By November 2009 the state was on its way to meeting the target. Hydrogen stations were established along approximately 500 miles of freeway, as far south as Chula Vista and as far north as Sacramento. The state had more hydrogen fueling stations, by far, than any other state. Nearly half, or 38, of the 86 hydrogen fueling stations in the country in November 2009 were located in California.[4] New York and Michigan were next with 9 and 8 hydrogen fueling stations, respectively.[5]

In February 2009, Steven Chu, the U.S. secretary of energy under President Barack Obama, issued a statement that more than likely displeased California. Chu said the Department of Energy was scaling back its funding for hydrogen and fuel cell research. The federal government had provided substantial funding for fuel cells and hydrogen under the administration of George W. Bush. But Chu felt hydrogen had too many barriers, such as infrastructure difficulties and the challenges inherent in storing hydrogen in vehicles, to be viable. In an interview with *Technology Review* a few months after his statement Chu observes,

> I always was somewhat skeptical of it [hydrogen] because, right now, the way we get hydrogen primarily is from reforming [natural] gas. That's not an ideal source of hydrogen. You're giving away some of the energy content of natural gas, which is a very valuable fuel. So that's one problem. The other problem is, if it's for transportation, we don't have a good storage mechanism yet. What else? The fuel cells aren't there yet, and the distribution infrastructure isn't there yet. So you have four things that have to happen all at once. And so it always

Space-Based Solar Power

Consistent with the U.S. National Security Strategy, energy and environmental security are not just problems for America, they are critical challenges for the entire world. Expanding human populations and declining natural resources are potential sources of local and strategic conflict in the twenty-first century, and many see energy scarcity as the foremost threat to national security. Conflict prevention is of particular interest to security-providing institutions such as the U.S. Department of Defense, which has elevated energy and environmental security as priority issues with a mandate to proactively find and create solutions that ensure U.S. and partner strategic security is preserved.

The magnitude of the looming energy and environmental problems is significant enough to warrant consideration of all options, to include revisiting a concept called Space-Based Solar Power (SBSP), first invented in the United States almost 40 years ago. The basic idea is very straightforward: place very large solar arrays into continuously and intensely sunlit Earth orbit (1,366 watts/sq. m), collect gigawatts of electrical energy, electromagnetically beam it to Earth, and receive it on the surface for use . . . as baseload power via direct connection to the existing electrical grid, conversion into manufactured synthetic hydrocarbon fuels, or as low-intensity broadcast power beamed directly to consumers. A single kilometer-wide band of geosynchronous Earth orbit experiences enough solar flux in one year to nearly equal the amount of energy contained within all known recoverable conventional oil reserves on Earth today. This amount of energy indicates that there is enormous potential for energy security, economic development, improved environmental stewardship, advancement of general space faring, and overall national security for those nations who construct and possess a SBSP capability.

SOURCE: **Space Based Solar Power as an Opportunity for Strategic Security, Report to the Director, National Security Space Office, Interim Assessment, Release 0.1, October 10, 2007.**

looked like it was going to be [a technology for] the distant future.[6]

Fuel cell and hydrogen supporters disagreed with Secretary Chu's pessimism about hydrogen. In response to Chu's statement the National Hydrogen Association and the U.S. Fuel Cell Council issued the following joint statement: "Fuel cell vehicles are not a science experiment. These are real vehicles with real marketability and real benefits."[7]

Inarguably, moving to a hydrogen economy poses several challenges, which depending on one's point of view, may take a short or a long time to address. There is another type of decarbonized economy that may not need as many radical changes to implement, however.

The Bioeconomy

Plants and organic wastes, or biomass, such as certain trees and grasses, wood and agricultural wastes, municipal trash, food waste, and animal manure can be used to generate both energy and products in what is called a bioeconomy. In a bioeconomy, animal manure and other wastes would be used to generate electricity and heat, while ethanol and biodiesel—a form of diesel fuel made from used grease or soybeans—would provide transportation fuels. Biomass-generated energy is generally considered climate friendly, even though there are carbon dioxide emissions associated with its use. That is because biomass is grown or otherwise created using carbon dioxide from the air. Therefore, when it is converted into energy, its carbon dioxide emissions are not contributing any additional amounts to the atmosphere. Fossil fuels, in contrast, emit carbon dioxide from carbon that was stored deep underground for millions of years. These emissions represent a net addition of carbon dioxide to the atmosphere.

Biorefineries are the cornerstone of the bioeconomy. Biorefineries are much like oil refineries. They can pump out several different fuels for energy use and a multitude of raw materials that can be used in the manufacturing sector. Instead of using petroleum to create fuels and products, however, biorefineries use biomass. The biorefinery concept is relatively new, and it has not been fully demonstrated yet. It is envisioned, though, that the main products of a biorefinery would be the transportation fuels ethanol and biodiesel. In addition to transportation fuels, biorefineries would produce plastics, fine chemicals, medicines, foods, biopolymers, cosmetics, and many other products—just like oil refineries do today.

The U.S. government has generally supported the bioeconomy concept. In 2005, the U.S. Department of Energy and the U.S. Department of Agriculture issued a report claiming that the nation could produce enough biomass—roughly a billion tons—to displace 30 percent of U.S. petroleum consumption.[8] According to Oak Ridge National Laboratory scientist Jonathan Mielenz, the report provided proof that a bioeconomy—anchored with biorefineries—is possible and that the U.S. government should provide funds to make it a reality. Said Mielenz, "the study was a critical contribution because it provided evidence for the biomass ethanol and chemical industries that a real and substantial resource base could be potentially available from which to build their businesses. This knowledge gave decision makers in government and elsewhere credible arguments to support funding and policy decisions needed for a fledgling biorefinery industry."[9] In 2008, the last year of the George W. Bush administration, the Department of Energy issued nearly $200 million in federal grants to small-scale biorefinery projects. On May 5, 2009, President Barack Obama announced plans to invest $786.5 million from the American Reinvestment and Recovery Act to provide funding for biorefineries and biofuels.

A large group of environmental and social organizations oppose the concept of a bioeconomy. They think it is an ill-conceived notion that will worsen climate change by causing the destruction of large amounts of forests to make way for agricultural land. In January 2009, organizations such as the Global

Justice Ecology Project, Food First, the Native Forest Council, Family Farm Defenders, the Rainforest Action Network, and several others, published an open letter warning of the dangers of industrially produced biofuels (the letter calls them agrofuels). It states, "Agrofuels are a false solution and a dangerous distraction and they must be halted. The continued pursuit of agrofuels will aggravate severely rather than resolve the multiple and dire consequences of the climate, energy, food, economic and ecological crises we face."[10] Another organization opposed to agrofuels is Grain, an international nonprofit organization working on behalf of small landowners. It contends that supporters of a bioeconomy do not care about preventing climate change. According to Grain, "the bottom line is that agrofuels are a new way for corporations, speculators and powerful agro-barons to make more money, sell more commodities, and consolidate their control over the earth."[11]

As the first decade of the twenty-first century comes to a close, there is no consensus on what a decarbonized economy will, or *should*, look like. Carbonaceous fuels still provide the vast majority of energy and products used in the world. When the last decade of the twenty-first century comes to a close, however, carbon may no longer be king. Hydrogen, biomass, or some other energy source may fuel the American and the world economies.

Notes

1. Quoted in Russell Fortmeyer, "Moving Away from a Carbon Economy," *BusinessWeek*, November 9, 2007.
2. Jeremy Rifkin, "The Third Industrial Revolution: Leading the Way to a Green Energy Era and a Hydrogen Economy," lecture. www.foet.org.
3. Arnold Schwarzenegger, Executive Order S-7-04, April 20, 2004. www.hydrogen highway.ca.gov.
4. Fuel Cells 2000, "Worldwide Hydrogen Fueling Stations," updated November 2009. www.fuelcells.org.
5. Fuel Cells 2000, "Worldwide Hydrogen Fueling Stations," updated November 2009.
6. Quoted in Kevin Bullis, "Q and A: Steven Chu," *Technology Review*, May 14, 2009. www.technologyreview.com.
7. California Air Resources Board, "California Hydrogen Highway Network CaH2Net— Summer 2009 Update." www.hydrogenhighway.ca.gov.

8. Bob Perlack et al., *Biomass as Feedstock for a Bioenergy and Bioproducts Industry: The Technical Feasibility of a Billion-Ton Annual Supply*, Washington, DC: U.S. Department of Energy and Department of Agriculture, 2005.

9. Quoted in Carolyn Krause, "The Billion Ton Study," *Oak Ridge National Laboratory Review*, 2007. www.ornl.gov.

10. Food First, "'Next Generation Biofuels': Bursting the New 'Green' Bubble Letter Challenges Unrealistic Promises from an Unsustainable Industry," January 15, 2009. www .foodfirst.org.

11. GRAIN, "Corporate Power—Agrofuels and the Expansion of Agribusiness," *Seedling*, July 2007. www.grain.org.

CHAPTER 11

Adapting to Climate Change

Apolar bear perched precariously atop a single block of ice floating alone in arctic waters is an image that has come to symbolize the effects of climate change. The polar bear is a dramatic representation of the harmful consequences of climate change. There are many other potential effects of a warmed Earth, however. Melting ice sheets could contribute to a dramatic rise in sea levels and threaten coastal communities. Water supplies may be affected, and drinking water may become scarce. Changes in weather patterns may damage crops and livestock and cause more human disease outbreaks. In order to survive, humans, wildlife, fish, plants, and entire ecosystems may be forced to change and adapt to an Earth transformed by climate change.

One of the most important government roles in responding to climate change is to help the planet and its inhabitants adapt to an altered Earth. The Intergovernmental Panel on Climate Change defines adaptation as "an adjustment in natural or human systems in response to actual or expected climatic stimuli or their effects, which moderates harm or exploits beneficial opportunities."[1] Government adaptation strategies for natural systems would help fish, wildlife, plants, and entire ecosystems withstand an altered climate. For example, certain species may adapt to climate change by migrating to cooler climates. The government can help these species adapt by protecting and enhancing migration corridors. Government adaptation strategies for human systems include shoreline protection to prevent sea-level rise from inundating low-lying coastal property or helping farmers adopt new farming practices. The role of government in confronting climate change, which initially focused only on reducing greenhouse gases, has expanded and evolved to include climate change adaptation strategies.

Helping Ecosystems and Wildlife Adapt

The U.S. government controls more than 600 million acres (243 million hectares) of land and more than 150,000 square miles of protected waters. The fish, wildlife, natural resources, and ecosystems within this land and water are managed by several agencies within the U.S. Department of Interior and by the National Oceanic and Atmospheric Administration, an agency of the U.S. Department of Commerce. In 2009, the secretary of the interior, Ken Salazar, issued an order requiring each bureau and office within the Department of the Interior, such as the U.S. Fish and Wildlife Service (FWS) and the Bureau of Land Management, to consider and analyze potential climate change impacts when developing management plans, setting research priorities, and making major resource decisions.

One of the most important government roles in responding to climate change is to help the planet and its inhabitants adapt to an altered Earth.

Helping ecosystems and wildlife adapt to a changed climate is a priority for the FWS, the nation's premiere conservation agency. In September 2009, it issued a draft strategic plan, called *Rising to the Challenge*, which set out the agency's strategy to respond to the impacts of climate change. In *Rising to the Challenge*, the FWS states that "we are committed to examining everything we do, every decision we make, and every dollar we spend through

GOVERNMENT OFFICIALS WEIGH IN ON ACTIONS TO ADDRESS CLIMATE CHANGE

How useful would the following federal government actions be in efforts to adapt to climate change?

	Very or Extremely	Moderately	Slightly or Not at All
Develop a National Adaptation Fund	82%	7%	8%
Issue Guidelines on How to Incorporate Adaptation into Existing Guidelines	64%	24%	9%
Creation of Campaign to Educate Public About Climate Change Adaptation	70%	19%	11%
Development of State and Local Climate Change Impact and Vulnerability Assessments	80%	14%	6%

Source: U.S. Government Accountability Office, *Climate Change Adaptation: Strategic Federal Planning Could Help Government Officials Make More Informed Decisions* (GAO-10-113), October 2009.

the lens of climate change."[2] The FWS also states that it will "act boldly, without having all the answers" and "make difficult choices, take calculated risks, and adapt to climate change."[3]

The FWS climate change adaptation strategy has several key elements. Chief among them are forming partnerships with other governments, monitoring climate impacts, and addressing non-climate threats along with climate change. To foster partnerships with state, local, tribal, and international governments, the FWS developed the concept of a Landscape Conservation Cooperative. Such cooperatives will focus on helping entire landscapes, which often extend across government boundaries, to adapt to climate change. To begin the process of quantifying the impacts of climate change, the FWS is creating monitoring and inventory programs. These programs will establish a baseline of data and help identify vulnerable species and ecosystems so governments can focus adaptation resources toward helping them. More than likely, vulnerable species are already facing threats from other stressors such as invasive species, environmental pollution, urban sprawl, and loss of wildlife habitat. The FWS adaptation strategy addresses these other threats too, because they can hinder the ability of natural systems to adapt to climate change. The FWS plan has been met with praise from conservation groups. According to Jamie Rappaport Clark, executive vice president of the Defenders of Wildlife in the United States,

> Global warming is forever changing the world and forever changing conservation. No longer can we rely on our past understanding of wildlife and ecosystems. The nation must chart a new way forward: first by developing a national climate change adaptation strategy for wildlife and natural resources; second by enhancing our scientific capacity; and finally, by providing the resources needed to address this enormous challenge. The release of this strategic plan shows the commitment of this administration to not only reduce global warming pollution but to also conserve wildlife and our environment for ourselves and generations to come.[4]

Creating Resilient Coastal Communities

More Americans live in coastal communities than in any other type of community. In 2005, approximately 153 million people, or 53 percent of the U.S. population, lived in counties along the nation's 95,331 miles (153,416 km) of ocean and Great Lakes coastlines.[5] People living in coastal communities generally depend on the ocean or lakes for their livelihoods. Fishing, marine transportation, energy facilities, recreation, and tourism are major industries in coastal communities.

Coastal communities are particularly vulnerable to many potential climate change impacts, such as sea-level rise and extreme weather events. Sea levels have been rising gradually for the last fifty years, and this could accelerate. Scientists predict that sea levels could rise by 3 to 32 inches (8 to 81 cm) by the end of the twenty-first century, depending on the amount of warming that occurs.[6] This rise could inundate low-lying coastal properties, destroy wetlands, erode beaches, contaminate freshwater sources with saltwater, and worsen flooding. Extreme weather-related events, such as hurricanes and cyclones, that may occur more frequently with warmer temperatures would also cause severe damage to large swaths of coastal areas.

Federal programs created in the 1970s and 1980s are helping coastal states devise climate change adaptation strategies. The U.S. Environmental Protection Agency's (EPA's) National Estuary Program was established by Congress in 1987. Estuaries, places where rivers meet the sea, are important components of coastal ecosystems. In January 2009, the National Estuary Program released a report outlining several strategies states and communities can implement, depending on their own particular circumstances, to protect their coastal communities from climate change impacts. Restoring and maintaining wetlands are key components of these strategies. Wetlands' ability to regulate and store large amounts of water can reduce the impacts of sea-level rise, as well as hurricanes and other storms. Coastal scientists maintain that the loss of wetlands along the Gulf Coast contributed to the scale of devastation caused by Hurricane Katrina in 2005. The National Estuary Program recommends strategies to restore wetlands and allow them to grow and move inland. Other adaptation options outlined in the report include encouraging people to move out of coastal floodplains and developing living shorelines to provide species habitat and control erosion.

In 1972, Congress enacted the Coastal Zone Management Act to "preserve, protect, develop and, where possible, to restore and enhance the resources of the nation's coastal zone for this and succeeding generations."[7] The act encouraged states to create coastal zone management programs that seek to balance economic development along coasts with environmental conservation. Many states are using their coastal programs to respond to climate change impacts. For instance, Maryland's Coastal Program developed a Sea Level Response Strategy to address sea-level rise and a Living Shoreline Stewardship Initiative to promote and encourage shoreline stabilization alternatives. Delaware, Maine, South Carolina, and many other state coastal programs are also devising climate change adaptation strategies.

Protecting Water Resources

Another act from the 1970s could help protect ocean and inland water from the impacts of climate change and greenhouse gas emissions. The Clean Water Act of 1972 is the cornerstone of surface-water-quality protection in the United States. The goal of the Clean Water Act is to restore and maintain the chemical, physical, and biological integrity of the nation's waters so that they can support "the protection and propagation of fish, shellfish, and wildlife and recreation in and on the water."[8] This landmark environmental act is responsible for cleaning up many of

---

Following pages: Maine is one of several U.S. states to initiate a coastal program to adapt to climate change. DEA/G. Sioen/De Agostini/Getty Images.

the nation's waterways that had become polluted with sewage and industrial discharge in the 1960s.

In December 2007, the Center for Biological Diversity sent a petition based on the Clean Water Act to the EPA, asking the agency to address the impacts of carbon dioxide on ocean waters. The environmental group contends that oceans are absorbing vast amounts of carbon dioxide emitted into the air from the burning of fossil fuels. The extra carbon dioxide is making the ocean more acidic—lowering its pH—and threatening the health of the entire marine ecosystem. The group argued that carbon dioxide is in effect "polluting" the ocean and, thus, the Clean Water Act requires the EPA to address it. In January 2009, the EPA responded to the request, and said it will begin an investigation to see if Clean Water Act regulation of ocean acidification is warranted.

Some environmental law experts think the Clean Water Act is particularly suited to address climate change adaptation. Climate change may affect water resources in a variety of ways, including by increasing water temperatures, increasing water pollution, decreasing water supplies, and increasing flood events. All these impacts would reduce "the chemical, physical, and biological integrity" of the nation's waters and, thus, under the Clean Water Act, the EPA and the states may be required to address them. According to Florida law professor Robin Craig, "President Obama's administration and the EPA should recognize and embrace the Clean Water Act as a relevant and potentially very powerful and helpful climate change adaptation tool."[9]

The state of California is already developing climate change adaptation strategies for its water resources. In October 2008, the California Department of Water Resources issued a report, *Managing an Uncertain Future*, which set forth the department's plan to make water management decisions with climate change impacts in mind. Many of the items in the report have been included in the state's comprehensive Climate Change Adaptation Strategy and in the 2009 California Water Plan. Increasing the efficiency of urban and agricultural water use is a key strategy recommended by the Department of Water Resources. One of the ways the department recommends this be achieved is by requiring that integrated regional water management plans (IRWMPs) include water efficiency and other climate change adaptation measures. IRWMPs are developed by a collaborative of counties, cities, and other local governments in a particular region. The concept of using IRWMPs has been embraced in the United States and around the world as an effective way to sustainably manage water resources. IRWMPs are central to California's climate change adaptation strategy to make water use more efficient. These plans will almost certainly affect the agricultural sector in California, which is a huge consumer of water.

Adaptive Farming Practices

Some of the predicted agricultural impacts of climate change include reduced water availability; flooding; droughts; heat waves; loss of crop quality and a reduction in yields; and increased threats from weeds, pests, and diseases. To adapt to climate change in the agricultural sector, California is proposing a number of policies to protect water supplies and improve irrigation efficiencies, to keep agricultural land free from the constraints of urbanization, and to help farmers anticipate and respond to opportunities and adversities resulting from climate change.

Research is an important component of California's and the U.S. Department of Agriculture's (USDA's) agricultural adaptation strategy. Research, particularly biotechnological research, can be used to identify and develop crops and even animals that are found to be resistant or better suited to climate change. Toward this end, California is supporting research to identify and develop crop varieties, cultivars, and mixes of crops capable of adapting to expected climate change. These research results can help farmers select crops and livestock that will be most likely to succeed in a warmed climate. The USDA Agriculture Research Service (ARS) is also devoting resources toward finding ways for agricultural systems to adapt to climate change: "We have to re-think everything from top to bottom to respond to the changes we face today and in the future. We need to look at plant and animal breeding; soil management; fertilizer practices; and management strategies for weeds, diseases, and insects."[10]

In October 2009, the Washington, D.C.-based International Food Policy Research Institute (IFPRI) issued the report *Climate Change Impact on Agriculture and Costs of Adaptation*. The report presents the results of an IFPRI analysis of climate change impacts on the agricultural sector throughout the world, the consequences for global food security, and the costs of adaptation measures. The report suggests that agriculture and human well-being will be negatively affected by climate change and that developing countries, particularly in South Asia, will be the hardest hit. According to the report, "climate change will have varying effects on irrigated yields across regions, but irrigated yields for all crops in south Asia will experience large declines."[11] The IFPRI analysis also found that climate change will increase the price of agricultural crops and meat, which will ultimately lead to an increase in child malnutrition. Based on these stark predictions, IFPRI recommends that the international community increase investments in agricultural productivity for the developing world, improve global data collection, support community-based adaptation programs, and increase funding for adaptation programs by $7 billion per year.[12] According to IFPRI, "These investments may not guarantee that all the negative consequences of climate change can be overcome. But continuing with a 'business-as-usual' approach will almost certainly guarantee disastrous consequences."[13]

Adaptation in the Developing World

The IFPRI report points out an important aspect of climate change adaptation: Developing countries will generally face more extreme climate change impacts, and at the same time they will generally have a harder time adapting to those impacts. For

Climate Change Refugees

Climate Refugees is the name of a documentary film produced by Americans Michael Nash, Justin Hogan, and Pat McConathy. The premise of the film is that within the near future, millions of people are going to have to leave their homes because changes in the earth's climate will destroy the basis for their livelihoods. Nash, Hogan, and McConathy produced the film in order to bring attention to the millions of people who are currently displaced by environmental catastrophes and the millions more who will be displaced by climate change. According to the film's Web site, "more refugees are now displaced by environmental disasters than by war," and estimates are that "between 150 million and 1 billion climate refugees will be displaced within the next four decades." The film is meant to put a human face on the dire circumstances facing climate refugees around the world. The South Pacific islands of Tuvalu and Kiribati are featured. According to the film's Web site, eleven thousand natives will soon be displaced as sea-level rise engulfs these islands. New Zealand has agreed to take some of the displaced islanders, if they are younger than 45 years old and have a profession. Individuals who don't meet these criteria will, says the Web site, have to "swim for their lives." Nash, Hogan, and McConathy hope that their film will raise awareness about the plight of climate refugees and compel the international community to devise laws that give them asylum and a helping hand.

instance, nations in Africa could face tragic famines caused by a lack of rainfall and low crop yields. Small island countries may see devastating storms, storm surges, and sea-level rise. Factors that make climate change adaptation more difficult in developing countries include illiteracy, poverty, lack of infrastructure, low technology, and weak institutions. A 2005 study assessed each country and ranked it according to their vulnerability and adaptive capacity to respond to climate change. Of the fifty-nine countries found to be most at risk, thirty-three were in sub-

Saharan Africa, five were small island states, and many of the rest were conflict or postconflict countries.[14]

The United States Agency for International Development (USAID) is focused on helping vulnerable countries meet the challenges of global climate change. USAID was created in 1961 to provide foreign nonmilitary assistance. USAID supports and promotes economic growth, agriculture and trade, health, democracy, and conflict prevention, and it provides humanitarian assistance in sub-Saharan Africa, Asia and the Near East, Latin America and the Caribbean, Europe, and Eurasia. According to USAID, "many of the goals of economic development are complementary to efforts to address the humanitarian consequences of climate change. Adapting is a matter of reducing exposure and sensitivity while building capacity."[15] USAID uses a wide range of approaches to help developing countries respond and adapt to climate change. For instance, USAID collaborated with the National Aeronautics and Space Administration, Department of the Interior, and USDA to establish the Famine Early Warning Systems Network and the Malaria Early Warning System. These systems will monitor Africa's climate and help to predict future famines and malarial outbreaks. These programs can strengthen African early-warning and response networks, increase local technical capacity, and help Africa respond to climate change impacts.

As can be seen from the previous discussion, responding to climate change is not a one-size-fits-all approach. Different countries, and different regions within countries, will face different adaptive challenges depending on their geography, climate, and economic stability. Many climate change adaptation strategies are based on existing approaches to protect wildlife, ecosystems, and shorelines and to conserve water and increase agricultural productivity. In addition to the adaptation strategies described above, there are many other strategies that focus on human health, protecting endangered species, forests, and energy infrastructure. Stephen Seidel, vice president for policy analysis at the Pew Center on Global Climate Change, maintains climate change adaptation must be integrated into the everyday policy decisions of government officials responsible for land, water, wildlife, agriculture, health, forests, and energy. Testifying in front of the U.S. House of Representatives Committee on Energy Independence and Global Warming in October 2009, Seidel said, "Only by mainstreaming adaptation considerations across all relevant programs will our nation be in a position to meet the challenges of unavoidable climate change."[16]

Notes

1. Martin Parry et al., eds., *Climate Change 2007: Impacts, Adaptation and Vulnerability. Contribution of Working Group II to the Fourth Assessment Report of the Intergovernmental Panel on Climate Change*, Cambridge, UK: Cambridge University Press, 2007, p. 869.
2. U.S. Fish and Wildlife Service, *Rising to the Challenge*, Revised Draft, September 21, 2009.
3. U.S. Fish and Wildlife Service, *Rising to the Challenge*.
4. U.S. Fish and Wildlife Service, "What Others Are Saying," updated September 23, 2009. www.fws.gov.
5. National Oceanic and Atmospheric Administration, *Population Trends Along the Coastal United States: 1980–2008*, March 1, 2005.
6. Mark Siddall, Thomas F. Stocker, and Peter U. Clark, "Constraints on Future Sea-Level Rise from Past Sea-Level Reconstructions," *Nature Geoscience*, July 26, 2009.
7. National Oceanic and Atmospheric Administration, "Coastal Programs: Partnering with States to Manage Our Coastline." http://coastalmanagement.noaa.gov.
8. U.S. Environmental Protection Agency, "Introduction to the Clean Water Act," updated September 12, 2008. www.epa.gov.
9. Robin Craig, "Climate Change Comes to the Clean Water Act: Now What?" *Washington and Lee Journal of Energy, Climate and Environment*, Winter 2009/2010.
10. Charles Walthall, "Forum: Managing Agriculture in a Climate of Change," *Agricultural Research*, November–December, 2009.
11. Gerald Nelson et al., *Climate Change Impact on Agriculture and Costs of Adaptation*, Washington, DC: International Food Policy Research Institute, updated October 2009.
12. Nelson et al., *Climate Change Impact on Agriculture*.
13. Nelson et al., *Climate Change Impact on Agriculture*.
14. Nick Brooks, W. Neil Adger, and P. Mick Kelly, "The Determinants of Vulnerability and Adaptive Capacity at the National Level and the Implications for Adaptation," *Global Environmental Change*, 2005, pp. 151–163.
15. U.S. Agency for International Development, "Report to Congress on the Needs of Developing Countries in Adapting to Climate Change Impacts Required by 684 (2) of the Consolidated Appropriations Act, 2008," August 2008, p. 17.
16. Stephen Seidel, "Congressional Testimony—The Federal Government's Role in Building Resilience to Climate Change," Pew Center on Global Climate Change, October 22, 2009.

CHAPTER 12

Government Climate Change Challenges

As 2009 came to a close, the U.S. government had many pressing policy issues on its plate. On December 1, 2009, President Barack Obama announced he was sending an additional thirty thousand troops to the war in Afghanistan. Congress was involved in an intense debate over health care reform proposals. Unemployment was at its highest level in more than twenty years, and many government officials were trying to figure what it would take to create more jobs. Amid these critical issues, there was one other: climate change. On December 7, 2009, the international community began meeting in Copenhagen, Denmark, to try to hammer out a new climate change treaty to replace the Kyoto Protocol. Back in the United States, the Waxman-Markey carbon cap-and-trade bill and a similar bill in the Senate introduced by senators Boxer and Kerry were cued up for debate after health care reform was resolved. Climate change is just one of many pressing issues governments are responding to.

Governing is a difficult job, even for the simplest of issues, and climate change is not a simple issue. It involves complex scientific concepts and far-reaching, long-term consequences. It involves people who are frightened about the fate of the planet and ones who are skeptical that climate change is real. Government actions to mitigate climate change may cause economic hardship for many people. Unmitigated climate change may have immense economic expense, however, as well as environmental and human costs.

Because the climate is a global public good, a coordinated global response is needed to address it. The only way to make a dent in climate change is if all countries—particularly those with large economies—recognize the threat and take actions to reduce greenhouse gases. Controlling greenhouse gases is costly, however, and countries that do not act to reduce their own emissions will still benefit from the reductions of other countries. This makes it difficult to achieve a global commitment to mitigate climate change. The Montreal Protocol and other international environmental treaties demonstrated that in the face of a compelling planetary threat, individual countries will act for the global public good. The United Nations Framework Convention on Climate Change (UNFCCC) and the Kyoto Protocol form the basis of the world's coordinated global response to climate change.

Governing is a difficult job, even for the simplest of issues, and climate change is not a simple issue.

The United States' international response to climate change has been conflicted at times. U.S. scientists were some of the first to warn that carbon dioxide was warming the earth. Government agencies such as the Department of Energy, the Environmental Protection Agency (EPA), and the National Aeronautics and Space Administration have been studying climate change for several decades. Many U.S. government policy makers have been, and some still remain, skeptical about whether climate change is human caused, however. The United States was involved in all the negotiations and discussions surrounding the UNFCCC and the Kyoto Protocol. Yet, under the administrations of presidents Bill Clinton and George W. Bush, the nation failed to ratify the Kyoto Protocol over concerns that China and India did not have to reduce their greenhouse gas emissions. The U.S. position has been that these countries, particularly China, emit as much as, if not more, greenhouse gases than the United States, and if U.S. emissions are reduced but these other countries' emissions are not, the United States will be put at an economic disadvantage. Meanwhile, the climate change policies of presidents Bill Clinton and George W. Bush have made way for the policy of Barack Obama.

The U.S. response to climate change within its own borders has been centered on whether carbon dioxide should be called an air pollutant. Under the statutory provisions of the Clean Air Act, the EPA has authority to regulate all air pollutants. Many people think carbon dioxide is an air pollutant due to its role in climate change. Other people wonder how the government can regulate a gas that is necessary for photosynthesis and is exhaled from humans and other animals with every breath. Government regulation of carbon dioxide is likely to come in the form of a carbon cap-and-trade program or a carbon tax. Both the Waxman-Markey bill and the Boxer-Kerry bill would establish a carbon cap-and-trade program for the United States. Many people think a carbon tax would be simpler and easier to implement, however.

As the federal government considers whether carbon dioxide is an air pollutant and debates carbon cap-and-trade legislation, some states have decided to act on their own. The governors of the northeastern states developed a regional carbon cap-and-trade program called the Regional Greenhouse Gas Initiative. California, meanwhile, sought to curb emissions of carbon dioxide from automobiles and enacted legislation capping greenhouse gas emissions at 1990 levels by 2020, which would bring the state in compliance with the Kyoto Protocol.

Greenhouse gas mitigation policies are intertwined with energy policy. Americans are dependent on fossil fuels to power automobiles, heat homes, and provide electricity for TVs, computers, and other electronics. Yet fossil fuels are the main culprit in climate change. Government policies to reduce emissions include promoting hybrid electric vehicles and ethanol in the transportation sector, energy efficiency programs and building codes in the building sector, and renewable energy and fuels in the electricity sector. All these policies are generally costly, however, and this causes many people to oppose them, particularly when the economy is down. There are some people who think the United States and the world should obtain energy in a dramatically different way than we do today. They think we should stop obtaining energy from carbonaceous fuels and instead look to some other energy source, such as hydrogen or biofuels.

Forestry and agriculture can play important roles in greenhouse gas mitigation. Trees absorb huge quantities of carbon dioxide, but deforestation is reducing their mitigating effect. Deforestation creates a double whammy for climate change: An important carbon dioxide sink is removed at the same time as carbon, which was stored in the forest, is released into the atmosphere. Many people think preventing deforestation is one of the most important ways to help reduce atmospheric carbon dioxide, and they want to see it given credit as a climate change mitigation technique under international climate change treaties. Cows, animal manure, and overfertilized soil from agricultural operations emit greenhouse gases that are several times more potent than carbon dioxide. Overall, however, these emissions are small when compared to carbon dioxide emissions from energy processes. Agriculturally produced biofuels, such as ethanol and biodiesel, can offset gasoline and diesel fuel and play a role in climate change mitigation.

Governments have generally focused on climate change mitigation. Climate change adaptation policies are growing in number, however. The vast majority of government climate change actions have been to reduce greenhouse gas emissions from transportation, buildings, energy, and agriculture, as well as to reduce deforestation. As the earth warms and impacts appear, however, governments are beginning to put more and more focus on climate change adaptation policies. Studies show that climate change impacts will not be evenly dispersed throughout the world. People in developing countries may see the worst climate change impacts, but they will probably be the least able to adapt to them.

Responding to climate change presents many challenges for policy makers. The ways in which governments respond to climate change are constantly evolving as climate science grows and as experience reveals what does and does not work. The actions governments can take are varied and innumerable, limited only by the creativity, willingness to act, and conviction of individuals working at all levels of government.

Glossary

adaptation Initiatives and measures to reduce the vulnerability of natural and human systems against actual or expected climate change effects.

anthropogenic Resulting from or produced by human beings.

atmosphere The gaseous envelope surrounding the earth.

biodiesel A type of diesel fuel produced from soybeans and other biomass that has fewer emissions than petroleum diesel.

biofuel A fuel produced from biomass, such as municipal solid waste, agricultural crops, trees, and plants. Examples of biofuel include ethanol and biodiesel.

biomass Refers to organic matter either living or dead, such as trees and plants, as well as municipal solid waste.

CAFE standards Refers to the Corporate Average Fuel Economy (CAFE) regulations in the United States, first enacted by the U.S. Congress in 1975, that are intended to improve the average fuel economy of cars and light trucks (trucks, vans, and sport-utility vehicles) sold in the United States.

carbon sequestration The process of capturing carbon dioxide and permanently storing it in deep underground formations or under the ocean to keep it out of the atmosphere.

Clean Air Act The federal law that regulates air emissions in the United States and gives authority to the Environmental Protection Agency (EPA) for protecting and improving both the nation's air quality and the stratospheric ozone layer.

clean coal Refers to technologies used to burn coal more efficiently, releasing significantly fewer gaseous emissions into the atmosphere.

deforestation The removal of forested land and its conversion into roads, agricultural land, or some other kind of nonforested land.

emissions trading A market mechanism that allows emitters (countries, companies, or facilities) to buy emissions from or sell emissions to other emitters.

energy efficiency A measure of how much energy is used by a system or device versus how much energy is wasted.

Energy Star A program started by the U.S. government in 1992 under which certain appliances are rated and given an Energy Star label for being very energy efficient.

ethanol An alternative automobile fuel produced using corn or other biomass.

feed-in tariff A government program that requires utilities to buy from renewable energy facilities at government-set prices.

fuel economy Refers to the relationship between the distance traveled by a vehicle and the amount of fuel it consumes.

global warming potential A measure of how potent a gaseous emission is at warming the earth.

greenhouse effect The process wherein certain gases in the atmosphere, that is, greenhouse gases, trap energy from the sun and warm the earth.

greenhouse gas Those gaseous constituents of the atmosphere, both natural and anthropogenic, that trap energy from the sun and warm the earth. The Kyoto Protocol refers specifically to the following six: carbon dioxide, methane, nitrous oxide, hydrofluorocarbons, perfluorocarbons, and sulfur hexafluoride.

hydrogen fuel cell A piece of equipment that converts hydrogen and oxygen from the air into electricity and water, without gaseous emissions.

integrated gasification combined cycle A type of clean-coal power plant.

Intergovernmental Panel on Climate Change (IPCC) A scientific body charged with providing the world a clear scientific view on the current state of climate change and its potential environmental and socioeconomic consequences.

Keeling Curve A graph showing the variation in concentration of atmospheric carbon dioxide since 1958, which is based on continuous measurements taken at the Mauna Loa Observatory in Hawaii under the supervision of Charles David Keeling.

Kyoto Protocol An international agreement adopted in December 1997 in Kyoto, Japan. The protocol sets binding emission targets for developed countries that would reduce their emissions on average to 5.2 percent below 1990 levels.

methane digesters Large tanks installed at farms to produce methane from animal manure and use it to generate heat or electricity.

mitigation Techniques or processes that reduce or offset the adverse impacts of climate change.

Montreal Protocol An international treaty designed to protect the ozone layer by phasing out the production of a number of chlorofluorocarbons (CFCs) and other substances believed to be responsible for stratospheric ozone depletion.

reforestation Planting of forests on lands that have previously supported forests but that were converted to some other type of land.

renewable energy Energy derived from a natural source that is renewable over a human lifetime, such as solar power, wind power, biomass power, or hydroelectric power.

renewable portfolio standard A government program that requires utilities to generate a certain amount of energy from renewable energy sources.

stratosphere An upper layer of the earth's atmosphere (about ten to thirty miles above the earth's surface), where ozone is important for protecting the earth from the sun's harmful rays.

United Nations Framework Convention on Climate Change (UNFCCC) A treaty signed at the 1992 Earth Summit in Rio de Janeiro that calls for the "stabilization of greenhouse gas concentrations in the atmosphere at a level that would prevent dangerous anthropogenic interference with the climate system."

For Further Research

Books

Andrew E. Dessler and Edward A. Parson, *The Science and Politics of Global Climate Change: A Guide to the Debate*. New York: Cambridge University Press, 2007.
> Provides an accessible primer clarifying the conflicting claims of the climate change debate. The authors describe the scientific and political processes associated with climate change.

Mickey Gjerris, Christian Gamborg, Jørgen E. Olesen, and Jakob Wolf, *Earth on Fire—Climate Change from a Philosophical and Ethical Perspective*. Copenhagen, Denmark: University of Copenhagen, 2009.
> A compilation of perspectives on climate change from researchers within the fields of science, the arts, and theology, the book aims to show how climate change raises not only a number of questions that can be answered within the scientific community, but in other disciplines as well.

Ingrid Kelley, *Energy in America: A Tour of Our Fossil Fuel Culture and Beyond*. Burlington: University of Vermont Press, 2008.
> Offers a concise yet comprehensive explanation of the key intersections of energy, the environment, the economy, and sustainability. The book provides a foundation for understanding how energy policy is closely intertwined with climate change policy.

George Monbiot, *Heat: How to Stop the Planet from Burning*. Scarborough, Ontario: Doubleday Canada, 2007.
> Contends that the question is no longer whether climate change is actually happening, but instead what to do about it. The author offers an ambitious and far-reaching program to cut carbon dioxide emissions to the point where the environmental scales start tipping away from catastrophe.

National Research Council, *Evaluating Progress of the U.S. Climate Change Science Program*. Washington, DC: National Academies Press, 2007.

Provides a progress report on the effectiveness of the U.S. Climate Change Science Program, created to deal with climate change issues.

Dianne Rahm, *Climate Change Policy in the United States: The Science, the Politics, and the Prospects for Change*. Jefferson, NC: McFarland & Co., 2009.

Examines the international agreements regarding climate change and the U.S. response to those agreements, and frames the scientific debate about climate change against moral, ethical, and religious considerations.

Burton Richter, *Beyond Smoke and Mirrors: Climate Change and Energy in the 21st Century*. New York: Cambridge University Press, 2010.

Provides a survey of the climate change problem and offers some viable solutions. The author focuses on energy policy and reviews all the world's major energy sources and their opportunities for improvement in the context of climate change. He warns that governments are largely falling far short in devising the required energy policies to address climate change.

David J.C. Shearman and Joseph Wayne Smith, *The Climate Change Challenge and the Failure of Democracy*. Santa Barbara, CA: Greenwood, 2007.

Presents evidence that the fundamental problem causing environmental destruction—and climate change in particular—is the operation of liberal democracy. The authors contend that climate change threatens the future of civilization, but humanity is impotent in effecting solutions.

Tavis Smiley and Stephanie Robinson, *Accountable: Making America as Good as Its Promise*. New York: Simon and Schuster, 2009.

Provides real-life examples of how crucial issues, including climate change, the environment, health care, and education, manifest themselves in communities. The book demonstrates the urgent need to hold politicians and ourselves responsible for dealing with these crucial issues.

David G. Victor, *Climate Change: Debating America's Policy Options*. New York: Council on Foreign Relations, 2004.

Offers three contrasting perspectives, each cast as a presidential speech, on how the government should respond to the complex issues associated with climate change.

Worldwatch Institute, *State of the World 2009: Into a Warming World*. New York: W.W. Norton & Co., 2009.
Provides in-depth and accessible information about the science, policy, and economic implications of climate change and suggests what the world needs to do to adapt to climate change.

Periodicals

Sharon Begley, "China and India Will Pay, Though Others Started Global Warming," *Newsweek*, August 27, 2009.

David Blanford and Tim Josling, "Greenhouse Gas Reduction Policies and Agriculture: Implications for Production Incentives and International Trade Disciplines," *International Food and Agricultural Trade Policy Council*, August 2009.

Keith Bradsher, "China Outpaces U.S. in Cleaner Coal-Fired Plants," *New York Times*, May 10, 2009.

Jane Braxton Little, "Carbon Equation," *Nature Conservancy Magazine*, Winter 2009.

Ronald Brownstein, "The California Experiment," *The Atlantic*, October 2009.

Doug Caruso, "State Shields Specifics of Weatherized Homes," *Columbus Dispatch*, October 19, 2009.

Dan Charles, "Leaping the Efficiency Gap," *Science*, August 14, 2009.

Richard Conniff, "The Political History of Cap and Trade," *Smithsonian*, August 2009.

Amanda Cuéllar and Michael Webber, "Cow Power: The Energy and Emissions Benefits of Converting Manure to Biogas," *Environmental Research Letters*, July 24, 2008.

Dieter Helm, "Sins of Emission," *Wall Street Journal*, March 13, 2008.

Leslie Kaufman, "Greening the Herds: A New Diet to Cap Gas," *New York Times*, June 4, 2009.

Kevin Knobloch, "Carbon Dioxide: Should EPA Wait on Congress?" *National Journal*, February 2, 2009.

Paul Krugman, "An Affordable Salvation," *New York Times*, May 1, 2009.

Joel Kurtzman, "The Low-Carbon Diet: How the Market Can Curb Climate Change," *Foreign Affairs*, August 25, 2009.

Alan I. Leshner, "Don't Let the Climate Doubters Fool You," *Washington Post*, December 9, 2009.

Alex Newman, "Cheers and Jeers at Copenhagen's Climate Conference," *New American*, January 1, 2010.

U. Niggli, A. Fliessbach, P. Hepperly, and N. Scialabba, "Low Greenhouse Gas Agriculture: Mitigation and Adaptation Potential of Sustainable Farming Systems," *Food and Agriculture Organization of the United Nations*, April 2009.

Kim Stanley Robinson, "Return to the Heavens, for the Sake of the Earth," *Washington Post*, July 19, 2009.

Katie Theoharides, Gerald Barnhart, and Patty Glick, "Climate Change Adaptation Across the Landscape," Association of Fish and Wildlife Agencies, Defenders of Wildlife, The Nature Conservancy, and National Wildlife Federation, February 10, 2009.

Bryan Walsh, "The EPA's Move to Regulate Carbon: A Stopgap Solution," *Time*, February 20, 2009.

George Will, "Bad Climate for Global Warriors," *Washington Post*, November 8, 2009.

Worldwatch Institute, "Worldwatch Report: Mitigating Climate Change Through Food and Land Use," 2008.

Internet Sources

Jesse H. Ausubel, "Decarbonization: The Next 100 Years," *50th Anniversary Symposium of the Geology Foundation*; Jackson School of Geosciences, University of Texas at Austin, April 25, 2003. http://phe.rockefeller.edu/AustinDecarbonization.

Glen Barry, "The Rainforest Movement Is Dead . . . Long Live the Old Forest Revolution," *Climate Ark*, February 21, 2010. www.climateark.org/blog.

David Biello, "Carbon Capture and Storage: Absolute Necessity or Crazy Scheme?" *Scientific American, 60 Second Science Blog*, March 6, 2009. www.scientificamerican.com/blog/post.cfm?id=carbon-capture-and-storage-absolute-2009-03-06.

Marion Koshland Science Museum of the National Academy of Sciences, "Global Warming Facts and Our Future." www.koshland-science-museum.org/exhibitgcc/responses01.jsp.

Roger A. Pielke, "The Folly of Magical Solutions for Targeting Carbon Emissions," *Yale Environment 360*, July 29, 2009. http://e360.yale.edu/content/feature.msp?id=2175.

Science Daily, "Reducing Greenhouse Gases May Not Be Enough to Slow Climate Change," November 11, 2009. www.sciencedaily.com/releases/2009/11/091111083055.htm.

Spencer Weart, "The Discovery of Climate Change," Center for History of Physics; American Institute of Physics. www.aip.org/history/climate/index.html.

U.S. Environmental Protection Agency, "Cap and Trade 101." www.epa.gov/captrade/captrade-101.html.

World Health Organization, *Climate Change and Health, Fact Sheet No. 266*, January 2010. www.who.int/mediacentre/factsheets/fs266/en.

Web Sites

U.S. Environmental Protection Agency, Climate Change Site (www.epa.gov/climatechange). EPA's Climate Change Site offers comprehensive information on the issue of climate change in a way that is accessible and meaningful to all parts of society—communities, individuals, business, states and localities, and governments.

Intergovernmental Panel on Climate Change (IPCC) (www .ipcc.ch). The IPCC is the international scientific body charged with providing government leaders with an assessment of climate change science. The Web site provides all the IPCC assessment reports, as well as a wealth of other data and information on climate change.

Pew Center on Global Climate Change (www.pewclimate .org). The Pew Center on Global Climate Change Web site provides information and insights on climate change from scientific, economic, technological, and political experts.

Index

About the Author

Jacqueline Langwith conducts policy research for the nonpartisan Michigan Legislative Service Bureau in the areas of biotechnology, health care, controlled substances, telecommunications, climate change, alternative and renewable energy, and the generation of electric power. She has a master's degree in biochemistry obtained from Michigan Technological University (MTU). Prior to her position at the bureau, Langwith managed the Plant Biotechnology Research Center at MTU, where she contributed to several research articles concerning the biosynthesis of lignin in woody plants, in publications such as the *Proceedings of the National Academy of Sciences*, *The Plant Cell*, and *Nature Biotechnology*.